LONGMAN
Preparation Course
for the
TOEFL® Test

iBT
WRITING

DEBORAH PHILLIPS

PEARSON
Longman

Longman Preparation Course for the TOEFL® Test: iBT Writing

Pearson Education, 10 Bank Street, White Plains, NY 10606

Staff credits: The people who made up the *Longman Preparation Course for the TOEFL Test: iBT Writing* team, representing editorial, production, design, and manufacturing, are: Rhea Banker, Angela M. Castro, Dave Dickey, Warren Fischbach, Pam Fishman, Nancy Flaggman, Patrice Fraccio, Lester Holmes, Katherine Keyes, Melissa Leyva, Lise Minovitz, Linda Moser, Michael Mone, Mary Rich, and Ken Volcjak.

Project editor: Helen B. Ambrosio
CD-ROM technical manager: Evelyn Fella
Text design adaptation: Page Designs International
Text composition: Page Designs International
Text photography: Hutchings Photography, Pearson Learning Group

Library of Congress Cataloging-in-Publication Data

Phillips, Deborah,
    Longman preparation course for the TOEFL(r) test : iBT writing /
Deborah Phillips. — [2nd ed.].
        p. cm.
    Previously ed. published as: Longman preparation course for the
TOEFL(r) test, 1st ed. 2006.
    Longman preparation course for the TOEFL(r): iBT will be published in
four separate volumes: writing , reading, speaking, and listening.
    ISBN 978-0-13-612657-7 (writing SB split)
    1. English language—Textbooks for foreign speakers. 2. Test of
English as a Foreign Language—Study guides. 3. English
language—Examinations—Study guides. 4. English
language—Rhetoric—Ability testing. I. Title.
    PE1128.P4458 2007
    428.0076--dc22

                                                    2007027706

PEARSON LONGMAN ON THE **WEB**

Pearsonlongman.com offers online resources for teachers and students. Access our Companion Websites, our online catalog, and our local offices around the world.

Visit us at **pearsonlongman.com**.

Printed in the United States of America
1 2 3 4 5 6 7 8 9 10—BAH—12 11 10 09 08 07

CONTENTS

WRITING INTRODUCTION

ABOUT THIS COURSE _____

PURPOSE OF THE COURSE

This course is intended to prepare students for the Writing section of the TOEFL® iBT (Internet-Based Test). It is based on the most up-to-date information available on the TOEFL iBT.

Longman Preparation Course for the TOEFL Test: iBT Writing can be used in a variety of ways, depending on the needs of the reader:

- It can be used as the *primary classroom text* in a course emphasizing preparation for the TOEFL iBT.
- It can be used as a *supplementary text* in a more general ESL/EFL course.
- Along with its companion audio program, it can be used as a tool for *individualized study* by students preparing for the TOEFL iBT outside of the ESL/EFL classroom.

WHAT IS IN THE BOOK

The book contains a variety of materials that together provide a comprehensive preparation course for the Writing section of the TOEFL iBT:

- A **Writing Diagnostic Pre-Test** for the Writing section of the TOEFL iBT measures students' level of performance and allow students to determine specific areas of weakness.
- **Language Skills** for the Writing section of the test provide students with a thorough understanding of the language skills that are regularly tested in the Writing section of the TOEFL iBT.
- **Test-Taking Strategies** for the Writing section of the test provide students with clearly defined steps to maximize their performance in this section of the test.
- **Exercises** provide practice of one or more writing skills in a non-TOEFL format.
- **TOEFL Exercises** provide practice of one or more writing skills in a TOEFL format.
- **TOEFL Review Exercises** provide practice of all of the writing skills taught up to that point in a TOEFL format.
- A **Writing Post-Test** for the Writing section of the test measures the progress that students have made after working through the skills and strategies in the text.
- Eight **Writing Mini-Tests** allow students to simulate the experience of taking actual tests using shorter versions (approximately 25–30 minutes each) of the Writing section of the test.
- Two **Writing Complete Tests** allow students to simulate the experience of taking actual tests using full-length versions (approximately 55 minutes each) of the Writing section of the test.
- **Scoring Information** allows students to determine their approximate TOEFL scores on the Writing Diagnostic Pre-Test, Writing Post-Test, Writing Mini-Tests, and Writing Complete Tests.
- **Skill-Assessment Checklists** and **Diagnostic Charts** allow students to monitor their progress in specific language skills on the Writing Pre-Test, Writing Post-Test, Writing Mini-Tests, and Writing Complete Tests so that they can determine which skills have been mastered and which skills require further study.

WHAT IS ON THE CD-ROM

The CD-ROM, with test items that are completely different from the questions in this book, includes a variety of materials that contribute to an effective preparation program for the Writing section of the TOEFL iBT.

- An **Overview** describes the features of the CD-ROM.
- **Skills Practice** for the Writing section provides students with the opportunity to review and master each of the writing language skills on the test.
- Eight **Mini-Tests** allow students to simulate the experience of taking actual Writing test sections using shorter versions (approximately 25–30 minutes each) of the Writing section of the test.
- Two **Complete Tests** allow students to simulate the experience of taking actual Writing test sections using full-length versions (approximately 55 minutes each) of the Writing section of the test.
- **Answers** and **Explanations** for all Writing skills practice and test items allow students to understand their errors and learn from their mistakes.
- **Skills Reports** relate the Writing test items on the CD-ROM to the Writing language skills presented in the book.
- **Results Reports** enable students to record and print out charts that monitor their progress on all skills practice and test items.
- A **Send Data** feature allows students to send their writing results to the teacher.

The following chart describes the contents of the CD-ROM:

SKILLS PRACTICE		TESTS	
Writing Skills 1–8	29 questions	Writing Mini-Test 1	1 question
Writing Skills 9–15	50 questions	Writing Mini-Test 2	1 question
		Writing Mini-Test 3	1 question
		Writing Mini-Test 4	1 question
		Writing Mini-Test 5	1 question
		Writing Mini-Test 6	1 question
		Writing Mini-Test 7	1 question
		Writing Mini-Test 8	1 question
		Writing Complete Test 1	2 questions
		Writing Complete Test 2	2 questions

AUDIO RECORDINGS TO ACCOMPANY THE BOOK

The recording program that accompanies this book includes all of the recorded materials from the Writing Diagnostic Pre-Test, Writing Skills, Writing Post-Test, Writing Mini-Tests, and Writing Complete Tests.

OTHER AVAILABLE MATERIALS

Longman publishes a full suite of materials for TOEFL preparation: materials for the paper TOEFL test and the iBT (Internet-Based Test), at both intermediate and advanced levels. Please contact Longman's website at www.longman.com for a complete list of available TOEFL products.

ABOUT THE TOEFL iBT

OVERVIEW OF THE TOEFL iBT

The TOEFL iBT is a test to measure the English proficiency and academic skills of nonnative speakers of English. It is required primarily by English-language colleges and universities. Additionally, institutions such as government agencies, businesses, or scholarship programs may require this test.

DESCRIPTION OF THE TOEFL iBT

The TOEFL iBT currently has the following four sections:

- The **Reading** section consists of three long passages and questions about the passages. The passages are on academic topics; they are the kind of material that might be found in an undergraduate university textbook. Students answer questions about stated details, inferences, sentence restatements, sentence insertion, vocabulary, pronoun reference function, and overall ideas.
- The **Listening** section consists of six long passages and questions about the passages. The passages consist of two student conversations and four academic lectures or discussions. The questions ask the students to determine main ideas, details, function, stance, inferences, and overall organization.
- The **Speaking** section consists of six tasks, two independent tasks and four integrated tasks. In the two independent tasks, students must answer opinion questions about some aspect of academic life. In the two integrated reading, listening, and speaking tasks, students must read a passage, listen to a passage, and speak about how the ideas in the two passages are related. In the two integrated listening and speaking tasks, students must listen to long passages and then summarize and offer opinions on the information in the passages.
- The **Writing** section consists of two tasks, one integrated task and one independent task. In the integrated task, students must read an academic passage, listen to an academic passage, and write about how the ideas in the two passages are related. In the independent task, students must write a personal essay.

The probable format of a TOEFL iBT is outlined in the following chart:

	iBT	**APPROXIMATE TIME**
READING	3 passages and 39 questions	60 minutes
LISTENING	6 passages and 34 questions	60 minutes
SPEAKING	6 tasks and 6 questions	20 minutes
WRITING	2 tasks and 2 questions	60 minutes

It should be noted that at least one of the sections of the test will include extra, uncounted material. Educational Testing Service (ETS) includes extra material to try out material for future tests. If you are given a longer section, you must work hard on all of the materials because you do not know which material counts and which material is extra. (For example, if there are four reading passages instead of three, three of the passages will count and one of the passages will not count. It is possible that the uncounted passage could be any of the four passages.)

REGISTRATION FOR THE TEST

It is important to understand the following information about registration for the TOEFL test:

- The first step in the registration process is to obtain a copy of the *TOEFL Information Bulletin*. This bulletin can be obtained by downloading it or ordering it from the TOEFL website at www.toefl.org.
- From the bulletin, it is possible to determine when and where the TOEFL iBT will be given.
- Procedures for completing the registration form and submitting it are listed in the *TOEFL Information Bulletin*. These procedures must be followed exactly.

HOW THE TEST IS SCORED

Students should keep the following information in mind about the scoring of the TOEFL iBT:

- The TOEFL iBT is scored on a scale of 0 to 120 points.
- Each of the four sections (Reading, Listening, Speaking, and Writing) receives a scaled score from 0 to 30. The scaled scores from the four sections are added together to determine the overall score.
- Speaking is initially given a score of 0 to 4, and writing is initially given a score of 0 to 5. These scores are converted to scaled scores of 0 to 30.
- After students complete the Writing Pre-Test, Writing Post-Test, Writing Mini-Tests, and Writing Complete Tests in the book, it is possible for them to estimate their scaled scores. A description of how to assess their writing to determine approximate scaled scores of the various Writing tests is included on pages 128–134.
- After students complete the Writing Mini-Tests and Writing Complete Tests on the CD-ROM, information allowing students to assess their writing and determine approximate scaled scores is provided.

HOW iBT SCORES COMPARE WITH PAPER SCORES

Both versions of the TOEFL test (the PBT or Paper-Based Test and the iBT or Internet-Based Test) have different scaled score ranges. The paper TOEFL test has scaled scores ranging from 200 to 677; the iBT has scaled scores ranging from 0 to 120. The following chart shows how the scaled scores on the two versions of the TOEFL test are related:

iBT Internet-Based Test	PBT Paper-Based Test	iBT Internet-Based Test	PBT Paper-Based Test
120	677	65	513
115	650	60	497
110	637	55	480
105	620	50	463
100	600	45	450
95	587	40	433
90	577	35	417
85	563	30	397
80	550	25	377
75	537	20	350
70	523		

TO THE STUDENTS

HOW TO PREPARE FOR THE TOEFL iBT

The TOEFL iBT is a standardized test of English and academic skills. To do well on this test, you should therefore work in these areas to improve your score:

- You must work to improve your knowledge of the English *language skills* that are covered on the TOEFL iBT.
- You must work to improve your knowledge of the *academic skills* that are covered on the TOEFL iBT.
- You must understand the *test-taking strategies* that are appropriate for the TOEFL iBT.
- You must take *practice tests* with the focus of applying your knowledge of the appropriate language skills and test-taking strategies.

This book can familiarize you with the English language skills, academic skills, and test-taking strategies necessary for the Writing section of the TOEFL iBT, and it can also provide you with a considerable amount of Writing test practice. A huge amount of additional practice of the English language skills, academic skills, test-taking strategies, and tests for the Writing section of the TOEFL iBT is found on the CD-ROM.

HOW TO USE THIS BOOK

This book provides a variety of materials to help you prepare for the Writing section of the TOEFL iBT. Following these steps can help you to get the most out of this book:

1. Take the Writing Diagnostic Pre-Test at the beginning of the book. When you take the Writing Pre-Test, try to reproduce the conditions and time pressure of a real TOEFL test.
   a. Take each section of the test without interruption.
   b. Time yourself for each section so that you can experience the time pressure that exists on an actual TOEFL test.
   c. Play the listening audio one time only during the test. (You may play it more times when you are reviewing the test.)

2. After you complete the Writing Diagnostic Pre-Test, you should assess and score it, and record your results.
   a. Complete the appropriate Skill-Assessment Checklists on pages 129–130 to assess the skills used in the test.
   b. Score your results using the Writing Scoring Criteria on pages 131–132.
   c. Record your scores on the Test Results charts on page 134.

3. Work through the presentations and exercises for the Writing section, paying particular attention to the skills that caused you problems in the Writing Diagnostic Pre-Test. Each time that you complete a TOEFL-format exercise, try to simulate the conditions and time pressure of a real TOEFL test. For writing, allow yourself 20 minutes to write an integrated writing response and 30 minutes to write an independent writing response.

4. When further practice on a specific point is included in an Appendix, a note in the text directs you to this practice. Complete the Appendix exercises on a specific point when the text directs you to those exercises and the point is an area that you need to improve.

5. When you have completed all the skills exercises for the Writing section, take the Writing Post-Test. Follow the directions above to reproduce the conditions and time pressure of a

real TOEFL test. After you complete the Writing Post-Test, follow the directions above to assess and score it, and record your results.

6. As you work through the course material, periodically schedule Writing Mini-Tests and Writing Complete Tests. There are eight Writing Mini-Tests and two Writing Complete Tests in the book. As you take each of the tests, follow the directions above to reproduce the conditions and time pressure of a real TOEFL test. After you finish each test, follow the directions above to assess and score it, and record your results.

HOW TO USE THE CD-ROM

The CD-ROM provides additional practice of the Writing language skills and iBT-version Writing tests to supplement the Writing language skills and Writing tests in the book. The material on the CD-ROM is completely different from the material in the book to provide the maximum amount of practice. You can now send your writing tasks from the CD-ROM to a server, and your teacher can receive this information in the form of a report. Following these steps can help you get the most out of the CD-ROM.

1. After you have completed the Writing language skills in the book, you should complete the related Writing Skills Practice exercises on the CD-ROM.

AFTER THIS IN THE BOOK	COMPLETE THIS ON THE CD-ROM
Integrated Tasks (Skills 1–8) Independent Tasks (Skills 9–15)	Integrated Tasks (Skills 1–8) Independent Tasks (Skills 9–15)

2. Work slowly and carefully through the Writing Skills Practice exercises. These exercises are not timed but are instead designed to be done in a methodical and thoughtful way.
   a. Complete a Writing task using the skills and strategies that you have learned in the book. Take good notes as you work on a task.
   b. Review your written response.
   c. Use the *Sample Notes* button to compare your notes to the sample notes provided on the CD-ROM.
   d. Use the *Sample Answer* button to see an example of a good answer and to compare your response to this answer.
   e. Complete the *Skill-Assessment Checklist* to evaluate how well you completed your response.

3. As you work your way through the Skills Practice exercises, monitor your progress on the charts included in the program.
   a. The *Results Reports* include a list of each of the exercises that you have completed and how well you have done on each of the exercises. (If you do an exercise more than once, the results of each attempt will be listed.) You can print the *Results Reports* if you would like to keep them in a notebook.
   b. The *Skills Reports* include a list of each of the language skills in the book, how many questions related to each language skill you have answered, and what percentage of the questions you have answered correctly. In this way, you can see clearly which language skills you have mastered and which language skills require further work. You can print the *Skills Reports* if you would like to keep them in a notebook.

4. Use the Writing Mini-Tests and Writing Complete Tests on the CD-ROM periodically throughout the course to determine how well you have learned to apply the language skills and test-taking strategies presented in the course. The CD-ROM includes eight Writing Mini-Tests and two Writing Complete Tests.

5. Take the tests in a manner that is as close as possible to the actual testing environment. Choose a time when you can work on a section without interruption.

6. Work straight through each test section. The *Sample Notes* and *Sample Answer* buttons are not available during test sections.

7. After you complete a Writing test, do the following:
   a. Complete the *Skill-Assessment Checklist* as directed. (You must complete the *Skill-Assessment Checklist* to receive an estimated score.)
   b. Review your written response.
   c. Use the *Sample Notes* button to compare your notes to the sample notes provided on the CD-ROM.
   d. Use the *Sample Answer* button to see an example of a good answer and to compare your response to this answer.

8. After you complete any tasks on the CD-ROM, send your writing tasks to your teacher. Click on SEND DATA from the Main Menu. Your teacher will provide you with a teacher's e-mail address and a class name to fill in.

TO THE TEACHER

HOW TO GET THE MOST OUT OF THE SKILLS EXERCISES IN THE BOOK

The skills exercises are a vital part of the TOEFL preparation process presented in this book. Maximum benefit can be obtained from the exercises if the students are properly prepared for the exercises and if the exercises are carefully reviewed after completion. Here are some suggestions:

• Be sure that the students have a clear idea of the appropriate skills and strategies involved in each exercise. Before beginning each exercise, review the skills and strategies that are used in that exercise. Then, when you review the exercises, reinforce the skills and strategies that can be used to determine the correct answers.

• As you review the exercises, be sure to discuss each answer and what makes it correct.

• The exercises are designed to be completed in class rather than assigned as homework. The exercises are short and take very little time to complete, particularly since it is important to keep students under time pressure while they are working on the exercises. Considerably more time should be spent in reviewing exercises than in actually doing them.

HOW TO GET THE MOST OUT OF THE TESTS IN THE BOOK

There are four different types of tests in this book: Writing Diagnostic Pre-Test, Writing Post-Test, Writing Mini-Tests, and Writing Complete Tests. When the tests are given, it is important that the test conditions be as similar to actual TOEFL test conditions as possible; each section of the test should be given without interruption and under the time pressure of the actual test.

Review of the tests should emphasize the function served by each of these different types of tests:

- While reviewing the Writing Diagnostic Pre-Test, you should encourage students to determine the areas where they require further practice.
- While reviewing the Writing Post-Test, you should emphasize the language skills and strategies involved in determining the correct answer to each question.
- While reviewing the Writing Mini-Tests, you should review the language skills and test-taking strategies that are applicable to the tests.
- While reviewing the Writing Complete Tests, you should emphasize the overall strategies for the Writing Complete Tests and review the variety of individual language skills and strategies taught throughout the course.

HOW TO GET THE MOST OUT OF THE CD-ROM

The CD-ROM is designed to supplement the practice that is contained in the book and to provide an alternate modality for preparation for the TOEFL iBT. Here are some ideas to consider as you decide how to incorporate the CD-ROM into your course:

- The CD-ROM is closely coordinated with the book and is intended to provide further practice of the skills and strategies that are presented in the book. This means that the overall organization of the CD-ROM parallels the organization of the book but that the exercise material and test items on the CD-ROM are different from those found in the book. It can thus be quite effective to teach and practice the language skills and strategies in the book and then use the CD-ROM for further practice and assignments.
- The CD-ROM can be used in a computer lab during class time (if you are lucky enough to have access to a computer lab during class time), but it does not need to be used in this way. It can also be quite effective to use the book during class time and to make assignments from the CD-ROM for the students to complete outside of class, either in the school computer lab or on their personal computers. Either method works quite well.
- The CD-ROM contains a Writing Skills Practice section, eight Writing Mini-Tests, and two Writing Complete Tests. In the Writing Skills Practice section, the students can practice and assess their mastery of specific skills. In the Writing Mini-Tests and Writing Complete Tests, the students can see how well they are able to apply their knowledge of the language skills and test-taking strategies to test sections.
- The CD-ROM scores the various writing tasks by counting the number of checkmarks on the Skill-Assessment Checklists. Scaled scores are assigned on the tests based on these checkmarks.
- The CD-ROM contains printable *Skills Reports* and *Results Reports* so that you can easily and efficiently keep track of your students' progress. You may want to ask your students to print the *Results Report* after they complete each exercise or test and compile the *Results Reports* in a notebook; you can then ask the students to turn in their notebooks periodically so that you can easily check that the assignments have been completed and monitor the progress that the students are making.
- The Writing tasks can be printed when they are written so that they can be reviewed and analyzed. Each of the Writing tasks is also automatically saved and can be accessed through the Results Menu. It is also possible for students to copy their Writing tasks into a word processing program so that they can make changes, corrections, and improvements to their Writing tasks.

HOW MUCH TIME TO SPEND ON THE MATERIAL

You may have questions about how much time it takes to complete the materials in this course. The numbers in the following chart indicate approximately how many hours it takes to complete the material[1]:

BOOK		CD-ROM	
Writing Pre-Test	2		
Writing Skills 1–8	12	Writing Skills 1–8	3
Writing Skills 9–15	12	Writing Skills 9–15	4
Writing Post-Test	2		
Writing Mini-Test 1	1	Writing Mini-Test 1	1
Writing Mini-Test 2	1	Writing Mini-Test 2	1
Writing Mini-Test 3	1	Writing Mini-Test 3	1
Writing Mini-Test 4	1	Writing Mini-Test 4	1
Writing Mini-Test 5	1	Writing Mini-Test 5	1
Writing Mini-Test 6	1	Writing Mini-Test 6	1
Writing Mini-Test 7	1	Writing Mini-Test 7	1
Writing Mini-Test 8	1	Writing Mini-Test 8	1
Writing Complete Test 1	2	Writing Complete Test 1	2
Writing Complete Test 2	2	Writing Complete Test 2	2
Appendix A	6		
Appendix B	6		
Appendix C	21		
	73 hours		**19 hours**

---

[1] The numbers related to the book indicate approximately how much class time it takes to introduce the material, complete the exercises, and review the exercises. The numbers related to the CD-ROM indicate approximately how much time it takes to complete the exercises and review them.

WRITING DIAGNOSTIC PRE-TEST

This section tests your ability to communicate in writing in an academic environment. There are two writing tasks.

In the first writing task, you will read a passage and listen to a lecture. Then you will answer a question using information from the passage and the lecture. In the second task, you will answer a question using your own background knowledge.

Integrated Writing Directions

For this task, you will read a passage about an academic topic. You have **3 minutes** to read the passage, and then the passage will disappear. Then you will hear a lecture about the same topic. You can take notes while you read and listen.

You will then write an answer to a question about the relationship between the reading passage and the lecture. Try to use information from the passage and the lecture to answer the question. You will **not** be asked for your personal opinion. You can see the reading passage again when you are ready to write. You can use your notes to help you. You have **20 minutes** to write your response.

A successful answer will usually be around 150 to 225 words. Try to show that you can write well and give complete, accurate information.

Remember that you can see the passage again when you write your response. As soon as the reading time ends, the lecture will begin.

Independent Writing Directions

In this task, you will write an essay that states, explains, and supports your opinion about an issue. You have **30 minutes** to plan, write, and revise your essay.

A successful essay will usually be at least 300 words. Try to show that you can write well by developing your ideas, organizing your essay, and using language accurately to express your ideas.

Questions 1–2

Question 1
Read the passage. On a piece of paper, take notes on the main points of the reading passage.

A truly amazing characteristic of human memory is that all people seem to experience a certain type of very specific amnesia, or the inability to remember events that have occurred in their lives. This particular kind of amnesia, which is apparently experienced quite universally, is the inability to remember events that took place in the first few years of life; even though the first few years of life are a time when learning is at its highest and tremendous amounts of information are learned, people seem to remember basically nothing from this period. When Freud first noted this interesting aspect of memory in 1805, he referred to it as **childhood amnesia**.

Since the time that Freud first noted this phenomenon, numerous studies have been conducted to learn about it, and the results of these studies are that people tend not to remember anything from the first three to five years of their lives. A possible difficulty in this type of study is that one cannot simply ask people if they remember events from the first five years of life because they may think that they remember things, but there is no way to check whether the remembered events actually occurred. Even when this difficulty is overcome in experiments, at least somewhat, by testing whether or not subjects can remember events that have been well documented from childhood, such as family celebrations or births of siblings, the results remain constant, that people tend not to remember anything from the first three to five years of life.

Listen to the passage. On a piece of paper, take notes on the main points of the listening passage.

Now answer the following question:

How does the information in the listening passage add to the ideas presented in the reading passage?

Question 2

Read the question. On a piece of paper, take notes on the main points of a response. Then write your response.

What recent news story has affected you the most? In what ways has it affected you? Use reasons and examples to support your response.

> Turn to pages 128–134 to *assess* the skills used in the test,
> *score* the test using the Writing Scoring Criteria, and *record* your results.

WRITING OVERVIEW

The last section on the TOEFL iBT is the Writing section. This section consists of two tasks, one integrated task and one independent task. You write your responses to these two tasks on the computer.

- The **integrated** task consists of a 250–300 word reading passage and a 1–2 minute lecture on the same academic topic. The information in the reading passage and the information in the listening passage are related, but the listening passage does not simply repeat what is in the reading passage. You take notes on the information in each of the passages, and then you must write a 100–200 word response about how the information in the two passages is related.

- The **independent** task consists of an essay topic. You must write an essay on the topic that is given. The ideas in your essay come from your personal experience rather than from material that is given to you.

Because these tasks are different, there are different strategies for each task. The following strategies can help you on the integrated task in the Writing section.

STRATEGIES FOR THE INTEGRATED WRITING TASK

1. **Be familiar with the directions.** The directions on every test are the same, so it is not necessary to spend time reading the directions carefully when you take the test. You should be completely familiar with the directions before the day of the test.

2. **Dismiss the directions as soon as they come up.** You should already be familiar with the directions, so you can click on Continue as soon as it appears and use your time on the passages and questions.

3. **Do not worry if the material in the integrated task is on a topic that is not familiar to you.** All of the information that you need to write your response is included in the passage. You do not need any background knowledge to answer the questions.

4. **Read the reading passage carefully.** You will have only a limited amount of time to read the passage.

5. **Take careful notes as you read the passage.** You should focus on the main points and key supporting material. Do not try to write down everything you read. Do not write down too many unnecessary details.

6. **Listen carefully to the passage.** You will hear the passage one time only. You may not hear the passage again.

7. **Take careful notes as you listen to the spoken material.** You should focus on the main points and key supporting material. Do not try to write down everything you hear. Do not write down too many unnecessary details.

8. **Organize your response very clearly.** You should have an overall topic statement that shows the relationship between the reading passage and the listening passage. You should also have a paragraph about the reading passage and a paragraph about the listening passage.

---

9. **Use transitions to make your response cohesive.** Your essay is easier to read and understand if you show how the ideas in your response are related.

10. **Stick to vocabulary, sentence structures, and grammatical points that you know.** This is not the best time to try out new words, structures, or grammar points.

11. **Monitor the time carefully on the title bar of the computer screen.** The title bar indicates how much time you have to complete your response.

12. **Finish writing your response a few minutes early so that you have time to edit what you wrote.** You should spend the last three to five minutes checking your response for problems in sentence structure and grammatical errors.

The following strategies can help you on the independent task in the Writing section.

STRATEGIES FOR THE INDEPENDENT WRITING TASK

1. **Be familiar with the directions.** The directions on every test are the same, so it is not necessary to spend time reading the directions carefully when you take the test. You should be completely familiar with the directions before the day of the test.

2. **Dismiss the directions as soon as they come up.** You should already be familiar with the directions, so you can click on Continue as soon as it appears and use your time on the passages and questions.

3. **Read the question carefully, and answer the question exactly as it is asked.** Take some time at the beginning of the task to be sure that you understand the question and what the question is asking you to do.

4. **Organize your response very clearly.** You should think of having an introduction, body paragraphs that develop the introduction, and a conclusion to end your essay.

5. **Use transitions to make your essay cohesive.** Your essay is easier to read and understand if you show how the ideas in your essay are related.

6. **Whenever you make a general statement, be sure to support that statement.** You can use examples, reasons, facts, or personal information to support any general statement.

7. **Stick to vocabulary, sentence structures, and grammatical points that you know.** This is not the best time to try out new words, structures, or grammar points.

8. **Monitor the time carefully on the title bar of the computer screen.** The title bar indicates how much time you have to complete your essay.

9. **Finish writing your essay a few minutes early so that you have time to edit what you wrote.** You should spend the last three to five minutes checking your essay for problems in sentence structure and grammatical errors.

WRITING SKILLS

The following skills will help you to implement these strategies in the Writing section of the TOEFL iBT.

INTEGRATED TASK

Writing Skill 1: NOTE THE MAIN POINTS AS YOU READ

In the integrated task in the Writing section of the TOEFL iBT, you will have to read an academic passage as part of the task. It is important for you to be able to read an academic passage of around 300 words in a short period of time. Look at an example of a reading passage that is part of an integrated writing task on hindcasting.

> **Reading Passage 1**
>
> It is common knowledge that **forecasting** is an attempt by meteorologists to determine what the weather will be like in the future. **Hindcasting** is the opposite of forecasting, an attempt to determine what the weather was like in the past. Meteorologists wish that records of the weather had been kept in full for at least a few millennia, but it has been only in the last century that detailed records of the weather have been kept. Thus, meteorologists need to hindcast the weather, and they do so by using all sorts of information from other fields as diverse as archeology, botany, geology, literature, and art. These pieces of information from other fields that are used as a basis for drawing conclusions about what the weather must have been like at some point in the past are called **proxies**.

As you read the passage, you should take notes on the topic and main points of the reading passage. Look at these notes on the topic and main points of the reading passage on hindcasting.

> TOPIC OF READING PASSAGE: hindcasting (trying to determine what the weather was like in the past)
>
> main points about the topic:
> * detailed weather records kept for less than a century
> * proxies (information from various other fields) used to hindcast weather

These notes show that the topic of the reading passage is *hindcasting,* which means trying to determine what the weather was like in the past. The main points about hindcasting are that *detailed weather records have been kept for less than a century* and that *proxies,* which are pieces of *information from various other fields,* are *used to hindcast weather.*

Now look at another example of a reading passage that is part of an integrated writing task on emotions.

Reading Passage 2

Humans all around the world, from culture to culture, seem to have a lot in common in terms of emotions. People from every corner of the world seem to express the same emotions: they all experience happiness and sadness, and they all experience anger and fear and surprise.

In addition to sharing the kinds of emotions they experience, people all around the world seem to use the same facial expressions to convey emotion. A facial expression that conveys happiness in the northern hemisphere of the world also does so in the southern hemisphere, and a facial expression that conveys anger in the eastern hemisphere also conveys anger in the western hemisphere.

These similarities in emotions around the world lead to the conclusion that the expression of emotions is something that is intrinsically natural in humans rather than something that is acquired from one's individual culture. That is to say, the expression of emotions seems to be natural throughout humanity rather than something that is learned in a specific culture.

As you read the passage, you should take notes on the topic and main points of the reading passage. Look at these notes on the topic and main points of the reading passage on emotions.

TOPIC OF READING PASSAGE: similarities in emotions from culture to culture

main points about the topic:
- same emotions around the world
- same facial expressions to show emotions around the world
- conclusion that emotions are intrinsic (natural)

These notes show that the topic of the reading passage is *similarities in emotions from culture to culture*. The main points about the topic are that people experience the *same emotions around the world,* that people use the *same facial expressions to show emotions around the world,* and that a conclusion can be drawn from this that *emotions are intrinsic, or natural.*

The following chart outlines the key information you should remember about dealing with the reading passage in the integrated writing task.

NOTING THE MAIN POINTS IN THE READING PASSAGE	
TOPIC	Make sure that you understand (and take notes on) the *topic* of the reading passage.
MAIN POINTS	Then focus on (and take notes on) the *main points* that are used to support the topic of the reading passage.

WRITING EXERCISE 1: Read each of the passages, and note the *topic* and the *main points* that are used to support each topic.

1. Read the passage. Take notes on the main points of the reading passage.

Homeschooling is becoming more and more popular in the United States. Parents who decide to homeschool their children keep their children out of traditional classrooms with one teacher and twenty to thirty or more children in each room. These parents educate their children by themselves in the home.

This move toward homeschooling does not seem to be best for the children who are homeschooled. For one thing, children in homeschools will not learn as much as children in traditional schools. This is because traditional schools demand that students learn a huge amount of material to pass from grade to grade. Homeschools are not set up in such a way that they can demand, as traditional schools do, that students master a certain amount of material before they pass on to a new level. For another, children in homeschools do not have much social interaction with other children. Children in homeschools do not have a classroom full of students to interact with, as children in traditional schools most certainly do. Children in homeschools generally have only a parent and perhaps a few siblings to interact with on a regular basis. Finally, children in homeschools will not have the broad curriculum that is available in traditional schools. Traditional schools offer a wide variety of subjects, more subjects than it is possible to offer in a homeschool. Traditional schools have an established and wide-ranging curriculum that cannot possibly be matched in a homeschooling environment.

TOPIC OF READING PASSAGE:

main points about the topic:

-

-

2. Read the passage. Take notes on the main points of the reading passage.

It is very common in English for one word to have many different meanings. This condition, where one word has different meanings, is known as **polysemy**. (This term comes from "poly-" meaning "many" and "sem-" meaning "meaning.")

"Sound" is one such polysemic word. As a noun, it refers to a noise (as in "a loud sound") or a body of water (as in "Puget Sound"). As an adjective, it can refer to a state of health (as in "sound mind and body"). It can also be an intransitive verb (as in "sound angry"), a transitive verb (as in "sound the alarm"), or part of a verb phrase as an outburst (as in "sound off") and an inquiry (as in "sound out").

You may think that the word "sound" is a truly wondrous polysemic word. After all, its definitions cover seven pages in one major dictionary and include 19 meanings as a noun, 12 meanings as an adjective, 12 meanings as a verb (some transitive and some intransitive), 4 meanings in verb phrases, and 2 meanings as an adverb.

But what about the extraordinary word "set"? It looks like such a short, simple word, only three little letters in all. However, if you look it up in an unabridged dictionary, you will find at least 57 meanings for "set" when it is used as a noun and over 120 meanings when it is used as a verb.

TOPIC OF READING PASSAGE:

main points about the topic:

-

-

3. Read the passage. Take notes on the main points of the reading passage.

Anthropologist Margaret Mead is known for her groundbreaking research on the effects of culture on gender roles. Her working hypothesis was that if gender behavior was the effect purely of biology, then what was considered masculine and feminine would be the same in all cultures. If gender behavior differed in different cultures, this would demonstrate that gender behavior resulted from culture rather than biology.

To test this hypothesis, Mead studied three different societies in New Guinea. The first society that she studied was the Arapesh. In this society, she observed that behavior by men and behavior by women were remarkably similar. She found that both men and women exhibited characteristics that are traditionally considered feminine: they were sensitive to each others' feelings and expressed emotions.

The second society that she studied in New Guinea were the Mundugumor, which was a society of headhunters and cannibals. The society was the opposite of the gentle and feminine Arapesh. In this second society, both men and woman exhibited characteristics that are traditionally considered male: they were harsh and aggressive.

In the third society that she studied, the Tchambuli, Mead found that males and females exhibited very different types of behavior. What was unusual was that the roles were the opposite of what we have come to expect. Mead found that in this society, the men were emotional and submissive to the women, and the women were dominant and aggressive.

Based on these findings, Margaret Mead came to the conclusion that culture, more than biology, determines gender behavior.

TOPIC OF READING PASSAGE:

main points about the topic:

-

-

Writing Skill 2: NOTE THE MAIN POINTS AS YOU LISTEN

In the integrated task in the Writing section of the TOEFL iBT, you will have to listen to an academic passage as part of the task. In this part of the integrated task, it is important for you to be able to listen to an academic passage of 1–2 minutes and take notes on the main points of the listening passage as you listen. Look at the following example of a listening passage that is part of the integrated writing task on hindcasting.

Listening Passage 1

(professor) *Now let me talk about how hindcasting was used in one particular situation. This situation has to do with the weather in seventeenth-century Holland. It appears, from proxies in paintings from the time by numerous artists, that the weather in Holland in the seventeenth century was much colder than it is today. Seventeenth-century paintings show really cold winter landscapes with huge snow drifts and ice skaters skating on frozen canals. Since it's unusual today for snow to drift as high as it is in the paintings and for the canals to freeze over so that skaters can skate across them as they are in the paintings, these paintings appear to serve as proxies that demonstrate that the weather when the paintings were created in the seventeenth century was much colder than it is today.*

As you listen to the passage, you should take notes on the topic and main points of the listening passage. Look at these notes on the topic and main points of the listening passage on hindcasting.

TOPIC OF LISTENING PASSAGE: paintings that are proxies showing weather in 17th-century Holland colder than today

main points about the topic:
- huge snow drifts higher than today's drifts
- skaters on canals that are not frozen today

These notes show that the topic of the listening passage is *paintings that are proxies showing* that the *weather in seventeenth-century Holland was colder than it is today.* The details in seventeenth-century paintings that show that the weather was colder are *huge snow drifts* that are *higher than today's drifts* and *skaters skating on canals that do not freeze today.*

Now look at another example of a listening passage that is part of the integrated writing task on emotions.

Listening Passage 2

(professor) *I'd like to talk now about the conclusion drawn in the reading passage, the conclusion that the expression of emotions seems to be natural, or innate, and is the same throughout all cultures. It is true, as the reading passage states, that certain aspects of emotion seem to be natural, or intrinsic, things like the kinds of emotions people express and the facial expressions people use to convey these emotions. But not all aspects of emotion are natural, or intrinsic, because some aspects of emotion differ from culture to culture. Let me talk about a few aspects of emotion that differ from culture to culture and are therefore learned, or acquired, rather than natural, or intrinsic.*

One aspect of emotion that differs from culture to culture is the trigger for specific kinds of emotion. By trigger, I mean the event or act that causes emotion. In various cultures, the triggers for emotions differ. Let me give you an example I think you can all identify with. Let's talk about humor, about what's funny. I'm sure you can understand that something that is funny in one culture just isn't funny in another culture. So, we see from this that what triggers emotion is different from culture to culture and is therefore acquired, or learned.

Another aspect of emotion that differs from culture to culture is the situational use of culture, that is, the situations where emotions are expressed. In some cultures, people do not express emotions openly, while in other cultures people do express emotions openly; for instance, in some cultures, men cry publicly, while in other cultures they absolutely do not. These cultural differences related to emotion show that these aspects are learned, or acquired, and are not natural, or intrinsic.

As you listen to the passage, you should take notes on the topic and main points of the listening passage. Look at these notes on the topic and main points of the listening passage on emotions.

TOPIC OF LISTENING PASSAGE: situations when emotions differ from culture to culture

main points about the topic:
- difference in triggers for emotion
- difference in situations where emotions are used

These notes show that the topic of the listening passage is *situations when emotions differ from culture to culture*. The main points about the topic are that there are *different triggers for emotion* in various cultures and that there are *different situations where emotions are used* in various cultures.

The following chart outlines the key information you should remember about dealing with the listening passage in the integrated writing task.

NOTING THE MAIN POINTS IN THE LISTENING PASSAGE	
TOPIC	Make sure that you understand (and take notes on) the *topic* of the listening passage.
MAIN POINTS	Then focus on (and take notes on) the *main points* that are used to support the topic of the listening passage.

WRITING EXERCISE 2: Listen to each of the following passages, and note the *topic* and the *main points* that are used to support the topic.

1. Listen to the passage. Take notes on the main points of the listening passage.

TOPIC OF LISTENING PASSAGE:

main points about the topic:

•

•

2. Listen to the passage. Take notes on the main points of the listening passage.

TOPIC OF LISTENING PASSAGE:

main points about the topic:

*

*

3. Listen to the passage. Take notes on the main points of the listening passage.

TOPIC OF LISTENING PASSAGE:

main points about the topic:

*

*

Writing Skill 3: PLAN BEFORE YOU WRITE

After you have noted the main points of the reading passage and the main points of the listening passage in the integrated writing task, you need to read the question and plan your response.

The question will be about the relationship between the main points of the reading passage and the main points of the listening passage. The question will most likely ask how the information in the listening passage either *adds to (supports),* or *casts doubt on (challenges),* or *contrasts (differs from)* the information in the reading passage. A listening passage may add to the reading passage by providing an example, or reasons, or causes. A listening passage may cast doubt on the reading passage by providing information that shows that the information in the reading passage is not correct.

Look at the following example of a question in the integrated writing task on hindcasting. In this example, the information in the listening passage adds to the information in the reading passage.

Question

How does the information in the listening passage add to the information in the reading passage?

You can see that the question is asking you to show how the information in the listening passage adds to the information in the reading passage.

To prepare a plan for your response, you should look at the notes you have taken on the reading passage and the notes you have taken on the listening passage. You should then think about how the ideas in the two passages are related. Look at a plan for the response on hindcasting.

Reading Passage = *a technique used by meteorologists*

TOPIC OF READING PASSAGE: hindcasting (trying to determine what the weather was like in the past)

main points about the topic:
- detailed weather records kept for less than a century
- proxies (information from various other fields) used to hindcast weather

Listening Passage = *an example of the technique*

TOPIC OF LISTENING PASSAGE: paintings that are proxies showing weather in 17th-century Holland colder than today

main points about the topic:
- huge snow drifts higher than today's drifts
- skaters on canals that are not frozen today

From this plan, you can see that the ideas in the reading passage and the ideas in the listening passage are related. The plan shows that the reading passage describes a technique used by meteorologists and the listening passage adds an example of the technique.

Now look at another example of a question in the integrated writing task on emotions. In this example, the information in the listening passage casts doubt on the information in the reading passage.

Question

How does the information in the listening passage cast doubt on the information in the reading passage?

You can see that the question is asking you to show how the information in the listening passage helps to show that the information in the reading passage is not accurate.

To prepare a plan for your response, you should look at the notes you have taken on the reading passage and the notes you have taken on the listening passage. You should then look at how the ideas in the two passage are related. Look at a plan for the response on emotions.

Reading Passage = *similarities leading to a certain conclusion*

TOPIC OF READING PASSAGE: similarities in emotions from culture to culture

main points about the topic:
- same emotions around the world
- same facial expressions to show emotions around the world
- conclusion that emotions are intrinsic (natural)

Listening Passage = *differences which cast doubt on the conclusion*

TOPIC OF LISTENING PASSAGE: situations when emotions differ from culture to culture

main points about the topic:
- difference in triggers for emotion
- difference in situations where emotions are used

From this plan, you can see that the ideas in the reading passage and the ideas in the listening passage are related. The plan shows that the reading passage describes similarities in emotions from culture to culture and the listening passage describes situations when emotions differ from culture to culture. The listening passage casts doubt on the conclusion in the reading passage by showing that emotions are not always similar from culture to culture.

The following chart outlines the key information you should remember about planning before you write in an integrated writing task.

PLANNING BEFORE YOU WRITE	
ADDING TO THE READING PASSAGE	The question may ask what the listening passage *adds* to the reading passage. This type of question may be worded in the following ways: How do the ideas in the listening passage **add to** . . . How do the ideas in the listening passage **support** . . .
CASTING DOUBT ON THE READING PASSAGE	The question may ask how the listening passage shows that the reading passage may not be accurate. This type of question may be worded in the following ways: How do the ideas in the listening passage **cast doubt on** . . . How do the ideas in the listening passage **challenge** . . .
CONTRASTING THE READING PASSAGE	The question may ask how the listening passage contrasts the information in the reading passage. This type of question may be worded in the following ways: How do the ideas in the listening passage **contrast** . . . How do the ideas in the listening passage **differ from** . . .

WRITING EXERCISE 3: Look at the notes that you prepared for the reading passages in Writing Exercise 1 and the listening passages in Writing Exercise 2. Read the question for each task. Then prepare a plan for your response.

1. How does the information in the listening passage challenge the information in the reading passage?

2. How does the information in the listening passage add to the information in the reading passage?

3. How does the information in the listening passage cast doubt on what is discussed in the reading passage?

Writing Skill 4: WRITE A TOPIC STATEMENT

After you have planned your response, you should begin writing your response with an overall topic statement. Your topic statement should show how the information in the reading passage and the information in the listening passage are related. It should also include the terminology *adds to, supports, casts doubt on,* or *challenges* from the question. Look at this information from the integrated writing task on hindcasting.

Reading Passage = *a technique used by meteorologists*

TOPIC OF READING PASSAGE: hindcasting (trying to determine what weather was like in the past)

Listening Passage = *an example of the technique*

TOPIC OF LISTENING PASSAGE: paintings that are proxies showing weather in 17th-century Holland colder than today

---

As you study this information, you should think about writing an overall topic statement that includes information about the topics of each of the passages and about how the two passages are related. Look at a possible topic statement for the integrated writing task on hindcasting.

Topic Statement

In this set of materials, the reading passage discusses a technique used by meteorologists, and the listening passage adds to this by providing an example of the technique from the 17th century.

You should notice that this topic statement does not include all the details about the topic and instead simply gives the overall idea. It also includes the terminology *adds to* from the question.

Now look at this information from the integrated writing task on emotions.

Reading Passage = *similarities leading to a certain conclusion*

TOPIC OF READING PASSAGE: similarities in emotions from culture to culture

Listening Passage = *differences which cast doubt on the conclusion*

TOPIC OF LISTENING PASSAGE: situations when emotions differ from culture to culture

---

As you study this information, you should think about writing an overall topic statement that includes information about the topics of each of the passages and about how the two passages are related. Look at a possible topic statement for the integrated writing task on emotions.

> **Topic Statement**
>
> In this set of materials, the reading passage cites some facts which lead to a conclusion, and the information in the listening passage cites facts which cast doubt on the conclusion in the reading passage.

You should notice again that this topic statement does not include all the details about the topic and instead simply gives the overall idea. It also includes the terminology *cast doubt* from the question.

The following chart outlines the key information you should remember about planning before you write in an integrated writing task.

WRITING A TOPIC STATEMENT	
RELATIONSHIP	The topic statement comes at the beginning of your response. This topic statement should show how the topic of the reading passage and the topic of the listening passage are related.
TERMINOLOGY	Be sure to include the terminology *adds to, supports, casts doubt on,* or *challenges* from the question in the topic statement.

WRITING EXERCISE 4: Look at the plans that you prepared for the integrated writing tasks in Writing Exercise 3. Then write a topic statement for each task.

1. In this set of materials, the reading passage _____

_____

_____ ,

and the listening passage _____

_____

_____ .

2. In this set of materials, the reading passage _____

_____

_____ ,

and the listening passage _____

_____

_____ .

3. In this set of materials, the reading passage _____

_____

_____ ,

and the listening passage _____

_____

_____ .

Writing Skill 5: WRITE SUPPORTING PARAGRAPHS ON READING PASSAGES

A supporting paragraph on the ideas in the reading passage should be very brief. It should state the topic and the main points of the reading passage as briefly as possible. Look at the notes on the reading passage on hindcasting and the supporting paragraph that is based on the notes.

TOPIC OF READING PASSAGE: hindcasting (trying to determine what weather was like in the past)

main points about the topic:
- detailed weather records kept for less than a century
- proxies (information from various other fields) used to hindcast weather

---

     The reading passage discusses the technique of hindcasting, which is a method used by meteorologists to try to determine what the weather was like in the past. According to the reading passage, detailed weather records have been kept for less than a century. As a result, meteorologists have been able to find out what weather was like in the past by using proxies, which are pieces of information from other fields.

As you read the supporting paragraph on the reading passage, you should note that it covers the topic and the main points of the reading passage very briefly.

    Now look at the notes on the listening passage on emotions and the supporting paragraph that is based on the notes.

TOPIC OF READING PASSAGE: similarities in emotions from culture to culture

main points about the topic:
- same emotions around the world
- same facial expressions to show emotions around the world
- conclusion that emotions are intrinsic (natural)

    In the reading passage, the author discusses some facts about emotions. These facts are that people around the world express the same emotions and that people around the world use the same facial expressions to show emotions. From these facts, the author draws the conclusion that emotions are intrinsic, or natural, rather than acquired, or learned.

As you read the supporting paragraph on the reading passage, you should again note that it covers the topic and the main points of the reading passage very briefly.

The following chart outlines the key information you should remember about writing supporting paragraphs on reading passages.

WRITING UNIFIED SUPPORTING PARAGRAPHS	
TOPIC	State the topic of the reading passage briefly.
MAIN POINTS	Summarize the key points of the reading passage briefly.

WRITING EXERCISE 5: Write supporting paragraphs on the reading passages for the integrated writing tasks that you worked on in Writing Exercises 1–4.

1. supporting paragraph on reading:

2. supporting paragraph on reading:

3. supporting paragraph on reading:

Writing Skill 6: WRITE SUPPORTING PARAGRAPHS ON LISTENING PASSAGES

A supporting paragraph on the ideas in the listening passage should be much more complicated than the supporting paragraph on the ideas in the reading passage. It should indicate the topic and the main points of the listening passage, and it should also relate the ideas in the listening passage to the ideas in the reading passage. Look at the notes on the listening passage on hindcasting and the supporting paragraph that is based on the notes.

TOPIC OF LISTENING PASSAGE: paintings that are proxies showing weather in 17th-century Holland colder than today

main points about the topic:
- huge snow drifts higher than today's drifts
- skaters on canals that are not frozen today

The listening passage provides an example of a situation where hindcasting was used. This situation involves proxies from the field of art to show what the weather was like in 17th-century Holland. Proxies from the field of art had to be used to determine the weather in 17th-century Holland because no weather records were kept from the past. The paintings that were used as proxies show that the weather in 17th-century Holland was much colder than it is today. There were details in the paintings that showed how cold the weather was. For example, there were huge snow drifts that were higher than today's snow drifts, and there were skaters skating on canals that are not frozen today.

As you read the supporting paragraph on the listening passage, you should note that it contains the topic and the main points of the listening passage and also refers to the main points of the reading passage. The information about hindcasting and proxies comes from the reading passage. The information about the specific example of paintings used as proxies to determine the weather in seventeenth-century Holland comes from the listening passage.

Now look at the notes on the listening passage on emotions and the supporting paragraph that is based on the notes.

TOPIC OF LISTENING PASSAGE: situations when emotions differ from culture to culture

main points about the topic:
- difference in triggers for emotion
- difference in situations where emotions are used

The listening passage casts doubt on the conclusion in the reading passage by showing that other aspects of emotions differ from culture to culture. While it is true that the kinds of emotions and the facial expressions used to show emotions are similar in different cultures, as the reading passage states, it is also true that the triggers for emotions and the situations where emotions are used differ from culture to culture, as the listening passage states. Based on the information in the two passages, the conclusion has to be drawn that some aspects of emotion are intrinsic, while other aspects of emotion are acquired.

As you read the supporting paragraph on the listening passage, you should again note that it contains the topic and the main points of the listening passage and also refers to the main points of the reading passage. The information about the situations when emotions are similar from culture to culture comes from the reading passage. The information about situations where emotions differ from culture to culture comes from the listening passage.

The following chart outlines the key information you should remember about writing supporting paragraphs on listening passages.

WRITING SUPPORTING PARAGRAPHS ON LISTENING PASSAGES	
TOPIC	State the topic of the listening passage.
MAIN POINTS	Summarize the key points of the listening passage.
RELATIONSHIPS	Relate the key points of the listening passage to the key points of the reading passage.

WRITING EXERCISE 6: Write supporting paragraphs on the listening passages for the integrated writing tasks that you worked on in Writing Exercises 1–4.

1. supporting paragraph on listening:

2. supporting paragraph on listening:

3. supporting paragraph on listening:

Writing Skill 7: REVIEW SENTENCE STRUCTURE

After you have written your response, it is important for you to review the sentence structure in your response. You should check the sentence structure of simple sentences, compound sentences, and complex sentences.

> NOTE: For a review of sentence structure, see APPENDIX B.

Look at the following sentences from a response about the development of a new theory.

Since a new theory was developed within the last decade.
   S   V

The reading passage explains a theory, the listening passage
      S   V   S
discusses the historical background of the theory.
   V

One issue that the lecturer points out it is that the main facts
    S   S V
contradict the theory.

The sentence structure of each of these sentences is not correct. The first sentence is an incorrect simple sentence. In this sentence, the subordinate connector *Since* in front of the subject and verb *theory was developed* makes the sentence incomplete. The second sentence is an incorrect compound sentence. In this sentence, the main clauses *reading passage explains . . .* and *listening passage discusses . . .* are connected with a comma (,), and a comma cannot be used to connect two main clauses. The third sentence is an incorrect complex sentence. In this sentence, the main subject is *issue* and the verb is *is*; there is an extra subject *it,* which makes the sentence incorrect.

The following chart outlines the key information you should remember about reviewing sentence structure.

REVIEWING SENTENCE STRUCTURE	
SENTENCE STRUCTURE	Check for errors in sentence structure in your response. Be sure to check for errors in simple sentences, compound sentences, and complex sentences.

WRITING EXERCISE 7: Correct the errors in sentence structure in the following passages. (The number in parentheses at the end of each paragraph indicates the number of errors in the paragraph.)

1.

Paragraph

1   In this set of materials, the reading passage discusses one type of management style, the listening passage presents the opposite type of management style. Both of the management styles they were proposed by Douglas McGregor. *(2)*

2   The reading passage discusses the theory X management style, which an authoritarian management style. What a theory X manager believes it is that employees dislike work and will try to avoid it. Since this type of manager believes that employees do not like to work. He or she must force employees to work, a manager must force employees to work with threats and punishment. *(4)*

3   The listening passage discusses a very different management style, it discusses the theory Y management style, which is a participative style of management. A theory Y manager believes that employees to work for enjoyment. Employees do not need to be threatened, they work for the pleasure of working. The role that this type of manager needs to follow it is to set objectives and then to reward employees. As they meet these objectives. *(5)*

2.

Paragraph

1   In this set of materials, the reading passage describes the different types of waves that occur during earthquakes and the listening passage explains how much damage each of these types of waves causing. *(2)*

2   According to the reading passage, three different types of waves they occur during an earthquake: primary (or P) waves, secondary (or S) waves, and surface waves. Primary waves are the fastest-moving waves, secondary waves are not as fast as primary waves. Surface waves resemble the ripples in a pond after a stone has been thrown in it, they are very slow-moving waves. *(3)*

3   According to the listening passage, the types of waves that occur during an earthquake they do not cause equal amounts of damage to structures. What causes most damage to structures during earthquakes it is surface waves. The really slow-moving surface waves cause most of the differential movement of buildings during earthquakes, and is the differential movement of buildings that causes most of the damage. Because the primary and secondary waves vibrate much faster and with less movement than surface waves. They cause little damage to structures. *(4)*

Writing Skill 8: REVIEW GRAMMAR

After you have written your response, it is important for you to review the grammar in your response.

> NOTE: For a review of grammar, see APPENDIX C.

Look at the following sentence from a response on a scientific phenomenon.

> Though scientists are quite sure that this phenomenon *exist,*
> *it's* causes are not so clear.

In this sentence, the verb *exist* does not agree with the singular subject *phenomenon;* to correct this error, you can change *exist* to *exists.* The contracted subject and verb *it's* in front of the noun *causes* should be changed to a possessive adjective; to correct this error, you can change *it's* to *its.*

The following chart outlines the key information you should remember about reviewing grammar.

REVIEWING GRAMMAR	
GRAMMAR	Check for errors in grammar in your response. Be sure to check for errors with nouns and pronouns, verbs, adjectives and adverbs, articles, and agreement.

WRITING EXERCISE 8: Correct the errors in grammar in the following passages. (The number in parentheses at the end of each paragraph indicates the number of errors in the paragraph.)

1. Paragraph

1   In this set of materials, the reading passage discusses attempt to deal with the problem of spelling in much words in American English; the listening passage explained why this attempt was not a successfully one. *(4)*

2   The reading passage explains that there is a problem in spelling a number of word in English where the spelling and pronunciation does not match; it then goes on to explain that philanthropist Andrew Carnegie made an efforts to resolve this. He gave an huge amount of dollars to establish a board calling the Simplified Spelling Board. As the name of a board indicates, its' purpose was to simplify the spellings of a words that are difficult to spell in English. Because of all of work that the board did, spellings like ax (instead of axe) and program (instead of programme) had become acceptable in American English. *(11)*

3   The listening passage explain why the work of the Simplified Spelling Board does not last. According to the listening passage, the main reason for the board's problems were that it went too far. They tried to establish spellings like yu (instead of you) and tuff (instead of tough). There was a real negative reaction to the attempt to change spelling too much, and eventually the board was dissolving. *(6)*

2.

▶ **1**   In this set of materials, the reading passage describes type of learning, and the listening passage provided an extending example of this type of learning. *(3)*

▶ **2**   The reading passage discusses aversive conditioning, which is define as learning involving an unpleasant stimulus. In this type of learning, an unpleasant stimulus is applying every times that a certain behavior occurs, in an attempt to stop the behavior. A learner can behaves in two different way in response to the knowledge that something unpleasant will soon occurs. Avoidance behavior is change in behavior before the stimulus was applied to avoid the unpleasant stimulus, while escape behavior is the opposite, a change in behavior after the application of the stimulus to cause them to stop. *(9)*

▶ **3**   The listening passage provides long example of aversive conditioning. This extended example is about the alarm in much cars that buzzed if the driver's seat belt is not fastened. In this example, the method of aversive conditioning that is applied to drivers are that every time a driver tries to drive with the seat belt unfastened, the buzzer went off. The driver exhibits avoidance behavior if he or she has fasten the seat belt before driving to avoid hearing the buzzer. The driver exhibits escape behavior if he or she attach the seat belt after the alarm had started to buzz, to stop the buzzing. *(8)*

WRITING REVIEW EXERCISE (Skills 1–8): Read the passage. Take notes on the main points of the reading passage.

Stonehenge is a huge structure located on the Salisbury Plain in the south of England. The main structure of Stonehenge consists of thirty upright stones, weighing twenty-six tons each, arranged in a circle, with thirty additional six-ton stones sitting on top of the upright stones. There is a second circle of stones inside the main circle, and this inner circle of stones is also composed of upright stones with additional stones atop the upright stones.

One of the most commonly held beliefs about the construction of Stonehenge is that Stonehenge was built by the Druids. The Druids were the high priests of the Celtic culture in England, and it has often been stated that the Druids had the structure at Stonehenge constructed in order to hold religious ceremonies there.

The idea that Stonehenge had been constructed by the Druids was first proposed by John Aubrey (1626–1697) in the seventeenth century. Aubrey, an antiquarian and scholar, came across the stone structure one day while he was out hunting with some companions. Over time, Aubrey became convinced that the structure had been created by the Druids. He included a chapter in his giant work *Monumenta Britannica* to advocate this idea about the creation of Stonehenge.

Dr. William Stukeley (1687–1765), an antiquarian and scholar who developed an interest in the Druids a century after Aubrey, was aware of the claims that Aubrey had previously made. Stukeley became deeply involved in the study of a possible relationship between Stonehenge and the Druids, and he strongly believed, as Aubrey had, that Stonehenge had been constructed by the Druids for use in religious ceremonies. Stukeley wrote the scholarly work *Stonehenge, A Temple Restored to the British Druids* (1740) to publicize his strongly held belief that Stonehenge was the work of the Druids.

Listen to the passage. On a piece of paper, take notes on the main points of the listening passage.

Now answer the following question:

How does the information in the listening passage cast doubt on the belief in the reading passage?

INDEPENDENT TASK

Writing Skill 9: PLAN BEFORE YOU WRITE

The first and most important step in the independent task in the Writing section of the TOEFL iBT is to decode the essay topic to determine what the intended outline is. Writing topics generally give very clear clues about how your answer should be constructed. It is important to follow the clear clues that are given in the topic when you are planning your answer. You will probably not be given too much credit for a response that does not cover the topic in the way that is intended. Study the following essay topic.

Essay Topic

Some people prefer to work in groups on projects, while other people prefer to work alone. What are the advantages of each, and which do you prefer? Use details and examples to support your response.

As you read this topic, you should quickly determine that the overall organization of your response should be an introduction, supporting paragraphs about the advantages of working in groups and the advantages of working alone on projects (with examples showing the advantages), and a conclusion. You should take a few minutes before you begin to plan your ideas. Study the following plan for an essay on the given topic.

INTRODUCTION:	advantages of working individually and in groups
SUPPORTING PARAGRAPH 1:	advantages of working in groups
(advantages):	• opportunity to learn from others
	• less work for individual members
(example):	• group project in history (four people, some know things others don't, one quarter of the work for each one)
SUPPORTING PARAGRAPH 2:	advantages of working individually
(advantages):	• previous success in working this way
	• enjoyment of doing work when and how I want
(example):	• individual project in history (working alone, doing work my way, getting good grade)
CONCLUSION:	• better for me to work individually

In this example, there are two advantages of working in groups and two advantages of working individually, and examples are provided.

The following chart outlines the key information that you should remember about planning before you write.

PLANNING BEFORE YOU WRITE	
HOW TO DECODE THE ESSAY TOPIC	Each topic in the independent task shows you exactly *what* you should discuss and *how* you should organize your response. You must decode the topic carefully to determine the intended way of organizing your response, and you must include an introduction and a conclusion.
HOW TO DEVELOP SUPPORTING IDEAS	Support your essay with the kinds of support that the essay topic asks for (such as *reasons*, *details*, or *examples*), and try to *personalize* your essay as much as possible. The more support you have, the better your essay will be.

WRITING EXERCISE 9: For each of the following writing topics, prepare a plan that shows the type of information you will include in each paragraph of the essay.

1. People have various ways of relieving stress. What are some of the ways that you find most effective in relieving stress? Give reasons and examples to support your response.

INTRODUCTION: *my ways of relieving stress*

SUPPORTING PARAGRAPH 1: *get away from the stress*
(examples): • *read a book, see a movie, visit friends*
(reason): • *necessary to leave stress to relieve it*
(personal story): • *a time last month when I was able to finish a difficult assignment after leaving it for a while and going to see a movie*

SUPPORTING PARAGRAPH 2: *get moving*
(examples): • *go for a walk, go dancing, go to the gym*
(reason): • *helpful in providing an outlet for stress*
(personal story): • *a time last year when I was finally able to deal with a problem with a friend after going on a long, long walk*

CONCLUSION: • *to relieve stress, get away from it and move*
• *problems seem small and solutions seem clear*

2. What famous place would you like to visit? Use details and reasons to support your response.

3. Do you agree or disagree with the following statement?

Actions speak louder than words.

Use specific reasons and examples to support your response.

4. Compare yourself today and yourself five years ago. In what ways are you the same or different? Use specific examples to support your response.

5. Some people prefer to play team sports, while others prefer to play individual sports. Discuss the advantages of each. Then indicate which you prefer and why.

6. What is the best age to marry? Give reasons and examples to support your response.

7. What are the characteristics of a good teacher? Use reasons and examples to support your response.

8. Do you agree or disagree with the following statement?

Haste makes waste.

Use specific reasons and examples to support your response.

9. It can be quite difficult to learn a new language. What do you think are the most difficult aspects of learning a new language? Give reasons and examples to support your response.

10. Do you agree or disagree with the following statement?

The TOEFL test is a wonderful test!

Use reasons and examples to support your response.

Writing Skill 10: WRITE THE INTRODUCTION

The purpose of the introduction is first to interest the reader in your topic and then to explain clearly to the reader what you are going to discuss and how you are going to organize the discussion. When finished with the introduction, the reader should be eager to continue reading your essay and should have an idea of what your topic is and how you are going to organize the discussion of your topic. You do not need to give the outcome of your discussion; you can save that for the conclusion. Study the following essay topic.

Essay Topic

Some people prefer to work in groups on projects, while other people prefer to work alone. What are the advantages of each, and which do you prefer? Use details and examples to support your response.

The following example shows one possible introduction to an essay on this topic.

INTRODUCTION

The educational system where I have been a student for the last 16 years is a system that places a high value on individual achievement and little value on group achievement. Having been a rather successful student in this educational system for the better part of my life, I am well aware of the advantages of working individually on projects. However, I can only imagine the advantages of working on projects in groups.

In the first part of the introduction, the writer provides background information that he or she has been a successful student in an educational system that is based on a lot of individual work, to interest the reader in the topic. By the end of the introduction, the reader also understands that the writer intends to discuss the advantages of individual work, based on personal experience, and then to discuss the advantages of working in groups from her or his imagination.

The following chart outlines the key information that you should remember about writing an introduction.

WRITING THE INTRODUCTION	
INTEREST	You should begin your introduction with information that will *interest* the reader in your topic.
TOPIC	You should state the *topic* directly in the middle of the introduction.
ORGANIZATION	You should end the introduction with a statement that shows the *organization* of the discussion of the topic.

WRITING EXERCISE 10: For each of the following writing topics, write introductions that include material to *interest* the reader in the topic, a statement of the specific *topic*, and a statement showing the *organization* of the discussion of the topic.

1.
> Some people prefer to work in one company for all their career. Others think it is better to move from company to company. Discuss the advantages of each position. Which do you think is better and why?

In my family we have experience both in staying with one company for a long time and in moving from one company to another. I find that one of these ways of working is better for me. However, each of these ways of working has its own advantages.

2.
> What famous place would you like to visit? Use details and reasons to support your response.

3.
> Do you agree or disagree with the following statement?
>   *Actions speak louder than words.*
> Use specific reasons and examples to support your response.

4.
> Compare yourself today and yourself five years ago. In what ways are you the same or different? Use specific examples to support your response.

5. Some people prefer to play team sports, while others prefer to play individual sports. Discuss the advantages of each. Then indicate which you prefer and why.

6. What is the best age to marry? Give reasons and examples to support your response.

7. What are the characteristics of a good teacher? Use reasons and examples to support your response.

8. Do you agree or disagree with the following statement?

   Haste makes waste.

   Use specific reasons and examples to support your response.

9. It can be quite difficult to learn a new language. What do you think are the most difficult aspects of learning a new language? Give reasons and examples to support your response.

10. Do you agree or disagree with the following statement?

The TOEFL test is a wonderful test!

Use reasons and examples to support your response.

Writing Skill 11: WRITE UNIFIED SUPPORTING PARAGRAPHS

A good way to begin writing effective supporting paragraphs in an independent writing task is to study your notes carefully before you begin to write. Then, as you write, you should think about introducing the main idea of each paragraph, supporting the main idea with adequate details, and connecting the ideas together in a unified paragraph (using cohesive techniques such as repeated key words, rephrased key ideas, pronouns and determiners for reference, and transition expressions).

> NOTE: For further work on cohesion, see APPENDIX A.

Look at the notes on the first supporting paragraph of the essay and the supporting paragraph that is based on the notes.

SUPPORTING PARAGRAPH 1: advantages of working in groups
    (advantages): • opportunity to learn from others
                 • less work for individual members
    (example): • group project in history (four people, some know things others don't, one quarter of the work for each one)

    The first point I would like to make is that there are strong advantages to working in groups. One benefit of this method of getting things done is that the members of the group can learn from each other. Something else that is good is that the work can be divided among the members of the group. If, for example, four people have to work in a group to get a 20-page paper done for history class, the paper can get done quickly. The reason for this is that different members of the group know different things and each group member has to write only 5 pages.

As you read the first supporting paragraph in the essay on working in groups and working individually, you should note that the first sentence of the paragraph is a topic sentence that indicates that the first supporting paragraph is about advantages of working in groups, and the rest of the sentences are details about this topic. You should also note the techniques that have been used to make the paragraph cohesive. The word *benefit* is a rephrasing of the key idea *advantages,* the word *group* is an example of a repeated key word, the phrase *for example* is a transition expression, and the word *this* is a pronoun that refers back to the idea *the paper can get done quickly.*

Look at the notes on the second supporting paragraph of the essay and the supporting paragraph that is based on the notes.

SUPPORTING PARAGRAPH 2:	<u>advantages of working individually</u>
(advantages):	• previous success in working this way
	• enjoyment of doing work when and how I want
(example):	• individual project in history (me working alone, doing work my way, getting good grade)

Though there are strong advantages to working in groups, there are some even more compelling advantages for me to work by (myself). I have had a lot of success working (alone), and (this) is because I enjoy working by myself, working when I want, and getting things done the way that I want. (Thus), if I had to write that 20-page history paper, I would rather do it myself, even though I would have to write all 20 pages, because I could do it the way that I want.

As you read the second supporting paragraph in the essay on working in groups and working individually, you should note that the first sentence of the paragraph is a topic sentence that indicates that the second supporting paragraph is about advantages of working individually, and the rest of the sentences are details about this topic. You should also note the techniques that have been used to make the paragraph cohesive. The word *myself* is an example of a repeated key word, the word *alone* is a rephrasing of the key idea *by myself*, the word *this* is a pronoun that refers back to the idea *I have had a lot of success*, and the word *Thus* is a transition expression.

The following chart outlines the key information you should remember about writing unified supporting paragraphs.

WRITING UNIFIED SUPPORTING PARAGRAPHS	
ORGANIZATION	Each supporting paragraph should include a sentence with the main idea of the paragraph and several sentences with supporting ideas.
COHESION	To make a supporting paragraph cohesive, you should use a variety of techniques, such as repeated and rephrased key ideas, pronouns and determiners, and transition expressions.

WRITING EXERCISE 11: Read the paragraph. Then answer the questions that follow.

English is not an easy language to learn. Of all the possible problems that I have experienced when trying to learn this language, the most difficult problem that I have encountered is that English does not seem to be spoken by Americans in the same way that it was presented in my textbooks. For instance, the first time that I asked an American a question, I got a strange response. The man who answered my question said something that sounded like "Dunno." I was sure that I had never studied this expression in my textbooks, and I could not find anything like it in my textbooks, and I could not find anything like it in my dictionary. I was surprised to learn later from a friend that this mysterious-sounding answer was really nothing more than a shortened version of "I do not know." Not too long after that I had an even more interesting example of my most difficult problem in learning English. One evening, I was unable to do some chemistry homework problems, so the next morning I asked a classmate if she had been able to do them. I was amazed when she gave the rather bizarre answer that the assignment had been a "piece of cake." I was not quite sure what a piece of cake had to do with the chemistry assignment, so I responded that I was not quite sure that the assignment really was a piece of cake. I have learned by now that she meant that the assignment was quite easy. Overall, I'm sure it is clear from these two examples what I find so difficult about the English language.

Repeated and rephrased key ideas

1. How many times does the key word "difficult" appear in the passage?
2. How many times does the key word "problem(s)" appear in the passage?
3. How is the phrase "strange response" rephrased in the passage?
4. How is the expression "Dunno" rephrased in the passage?
5. How is the word "surprised" rephrased in the passage?

Pronouns and determiners

6. What noun does the pronoun "it" refer to?
7. What noun does the pronoun "them" refer to?
8. What noun does the pronoun "she" refer to?
9. How many times is the determiner "this" used to refer back to a previous idea?
10. How many times is the determiner "these" used to refer back to a previous idea?

Transition expressions

11. Which transition expression shows that the first example will follow?
12. Which transition expression shows that the second example will follow?
13. Which transition expression shows that the summary of the main point follows?

Now write unified supporting paragraphs for the independent writing tasks that you worked on in Writing Exercises 9–10.

Writing Skill 12: CONNECT THE SUPPORTING PARAGRAPHS

To make sure your essay is as clear as possible, you should show as clearly as you can how the ideas in the supporting paragraphs in your essay are related. This can be accomplished (1) with a transition expression such as *the first, the most important,* or *a final way,* or (2) with a transition sentence that includes the idea of the previous paragraph and the idea of the current paragraph. It is best to use a combination of these two types of transitions. The following example shows how transitions can be used to show the relationships between the supporting paragraphs in an essay.

Essay Outline	
INTRODUCTION:	advantages of working in groups and individually
SUPPORTING PARAGRAPH 1:	advantages of working in groups
SUPPORTING PARAGRAPH 2:	advantages of working individually
CONCLUSION:	better for me to work individually
Transitions	
(to introduce SP1):	The first point I would like to make is that there are strong advantages to working in groups.
(to introduce SP2):	Though there are strong advantages to working in groups, there are some even more compelling advantages for me to work by myself.

The first supporting paragraph is introduced with the transition expression *The first point* to show that this is the first of the points that you are going to discuss in your essay. The second supporting paragraph is introduced with a transition sentence that shows how this paragraph is related to the previous paragraph; it includes a reference to the first supporting paragraph *strong advantages to working in groups* and a reference to the second supporting paragraph *more compelling advantages for me to work by myself.*

The following chart outlines the key information that you should remember about connecting the supporting paragraphs in your essay.

CONNECTING THE SUPPORTING PARAGRAPHS	
TRANSITION EXPRESSIONS	You can use transition expressions such as *the first, the next, in addition, another, finally* to connect the supporting paragraphs.
TRANSITION SENTENCES	You can use a transition sentence that relates the topic of the previous paragraph to the topic of the current paragraph.

WRITING EXERCISE 12: For each outline of an essay, write sentences to introduce each of the supporting paragraphs. You should use a combination of transition expressions and transition sentences.

1. INTRO: *a decision about whether or not to own a car in a big city*
   SP1: • the advantages of owning a car in a big city
   SP2: • the disadvantages of owning a car in a big city

   SP1: <u>The advantages of having a car in a big city are numerous.</u>

   SP2: <u>There may be numerous advantages to owning a car in a big city; however, there are also distinct disadvantages.</u>

2. INTRO: *the types of reading that I enjoy*
   SP1: • science fiction
   SP2: • romances
   SP3: • sports magazines

   SP1: _____

   _____

   SP2: _____

   _____

   SP3: _____

   _____

3. INTRO: *a preference for traveling alone or traveling in groups*
   SP1: • benefits of traveling alone
   SP2: • benefits of traveling in groups

   SP1: _____

   _____

   SP2: _____

   _____

4. INTRO: *characteristics leading to success as a student*
   SP1: • self-motivation
   SP2: • desire to succeed
   SP3: • joy in learning

   SP1: _____

   _____

   SP2: _____

   _____

   SP3: _____

   _____

5. INTRO: *living for today versus living for tomorrow*
    SP1: • people who have a philosophy of living for today
    SP2: • people who have a philosophy of living for tomorrow

    SP1: _____

    _____

    SP2: _____

    _____

6. INTRO: *my reasons for going to the movies all the time*
    SP1: • to be entertained rather than taught
    SP2: • to feel good rather than depressed

    SP1: _____

    _____

    SP2: _____

    _____

7. INTRO: *advice to someone trying to learn a new language*
    SP1: • listen to videos, television programs, radio programs in the new language
    SP2: • talk with native speakers of the language every chance you get
    SP3: • read newspapers, magazines, books in the new language

    SP1: _____

    _____

    SP2: _____

    _____

    SP3: _____

    _____

8. INTRO: *steps the government should take to protect the Earth's environment*
    SP1: • educate people about the causes and effects of environmental damage
    SP2: • create and enforce laws that penalize those who damage the environment
    SP3: • reward those who are environmentally conscious with tax incentives

    SP1: _____

    _____

    SP2: _____

    _____

    SP3: _____

    _____

Writing Skill 13: WRITE THE CONCLUSION

The purpose of the conclusion is to close your essay by summarizing the main points of your discussion. When finished with your conclusion, the reader should clearly understand your exact ideas on the topic and the reasons you feel the way that you do about the topic.

The ideas in your conclusion should be clearly related to the ideas that you began in the introduction. You should indicate what you intend to discuss in the essay in the introduction, and you should indicate the outcome or results of the discussion in the conclusion. Refer to the essay topic and sample introduction in Writing Skill 10.

Essay Topic

Some people prefer to work in groups on projects, while other people prefer to work alone. What are the advantages of each, and which do you prefer? Use details and examples to support your response.

The following example shows a possible conclusion to an essay on this topic.

CONCLUSION

I have worked individually throughout my education, and I have been successful working in this way because this style of work is a good match with my personality. I can imagine that, for some people, the cooperative benefits that come from working in groups might be a good thing. However, I prefer to continue with a style of work that has made me successful up to now. I hope that the success that I have had up to now by working in this way will continue to make me successful in the future.

Here the writer refers back to the personal information that was mentioned in the introduction, saying *I have worked individually throughout my education, and I have been successful working this way. . . .* The writer also briefly summarizes the advantages of each style of work by mentioning that working individually is *a good match with my personality* and that working in groups has *cooperative benefits.* Finally, the writer clearly states a preference for working individually because of the success that this style of work has brought *up to now.*

The following chart outlines the key information that you should remember about writing a conclusion.

WRITING THE CONCLUSION	
OVERALL IDEA	You should make sure that your *overall idea* is very clear.
MAIN POINTS	You should summarize the *main points* that you used to arrive at this overall idea.
INTEREST	You should refer back to the information that you used to *interest* the reader in the introduction.

WRITING EXERCISE 13: For each of the following writing topics, write conclusions that restate the main idea, summarize the main points, and refer back to the information that you used to interest the reader in the introduction.

1.
> Some people prefer to work in one company for all their career. Others think it is better to move from company to company. Discuss the advantages of each position. Which do you think is better and why?

From this, I think you can understand why I prefer to better my career by moving from company to company. I do understand that there are advantages in staying with one company for a long time; I certainly hear about these advantages from my family over and over. However, I have come to the conclusion that something different is better for me.

2.
> What famous place would you like to visit? Use details and reasons to support your response.

3.
> Do you agree or disagree with the following statement?
> > *Actions speak louder than words.*
> Use specific reasons and examples to support your response.

4.
> Compare yourself today and yourself five years ago. In what ways are you the same or different? Use specific examples to support your response.

5.
> Some people prefer to play team sports, while others prefer to play individual sports. Discuss the advantages of each. Then indicate which you prefer and why.

6.
> What is the best age to marry? Give reasons and examples to support your response.

7.
> What are the characteristics of a good teacher? Use reasons and examples to support your response.

8.
> Do you agree or disagree with the following statement?
>> *Haste makes waste.*
>
> Use specific reasons and examples to support your response.

9. It can be quite difficult to learn a new language. What do you think are the most difficult aspects of learning a new language? Give reasons and examples to support your response.

10. Do you agree or disagree with the following statement?
The TOEFL test is a wonderful test!
Use reasons and examples to support your response.

Writing Skill 14: REVIEW SENTENCE STRUCTURE

After you have written your essay, it is important for you to review the sentence structure in your essay. You should check the sentence structure of simple sentences, compound sentences, and complex sentences.

> NOTE: For a review of sentence structure, see APPENDIX B.

Look at the following sentences from an essay about a test.

Because the <u>test</u> in history class <u>was</u> extremely difficult.
          S   V

<u>I</u> finally <u>passed</u> the test, otherwise <u>I</u> <u>would have had</u> to take it over.
S   V   S   V

The <u>grade</u> that I intended to get <u>it</u> <u>was</u> much higher.
    S   S V

The sentence structure of each of these sentences is not correct. The first sentence is an incorrect simple sentence. In this sentence, the subordinate connector *Because* in front of the subject and verb *test . . . was* makes the sentence incomplete. The second sentence is an incorrect compound sentence. In this sentence, the main clauses *I . . . passed . . .* and *I would have had . . .* are connected with a comma (,), and a comma cannot be used to connect two main clauses. The third sentence is an incorrect complex sentence. In this sentence, the main subject is *grade* and the verb is *was*; there is an extra subject *it,* which makes the sentence incorrect.

The following chart outlines the key information you should remember about reviewing sentence structure.

REVIEWING SENTENCE STRUCTURE	
SENTENCE STRUCTURE	Check for errors in sentence structure in your response. Be sure to check for errors in simple sentences, compound sentences, and complex sentences.

WRITING EXERCISE 14: Correct the errors in sentence structure in the following passages. (The number in parentheses at the end of each paragraph indicates the number of errors in the paragraph.)

Paragraph

1 I definitely believe that taking part in organized team sports is beneficial. However, is beneficial for much more than the obvious reasons. Everyone recognizes, of course, that participation in sports provides obvious physical benefits. It leading to improved physical fitness, it also provides a release from the stresses of life. I spent my youth taking part in a number of organized sports, including football, basketball, and volleyball, as a result of this experience I understand that the benefits of participation much greater than the physical benefits. *(5)*

2 One very valuable benefit that children get from taking part in sports it is that it teaches participants teamwork. What any player in a team sport needs to learn it is that individual team members must put the team ahead of individual achievement. Individuals on one team who are working for individual glory rather than the good of the team they often end up working against each other. A team made up of individuals unable to work together often not a very successful team, it is usually a complete failure. *(5)*

3 What also makes participation in team sports valuable it is that it teaches participants to work to achieve goals. Playing sports it involves setting goals and working toward them, examples of such goals are running faster, kicking harder, throwing straighter, or jumping higher. Athletes learn that can set goals and work toward them until the goals accomplished. Is through hard work that goals can be met. *(6)*

4 By taking part in sports, can learn the truly valuable skills of working together on teams and working to accomplish specific goals. These goals not just beneficial in sports, more importantly, the skills that are developed through sports they are the basis of success in many other aspects of life. Mastering these skills leading to success not only on the playing field but also in the wider arena of life. *(5)*

Writing Skill 15: REVIEW GRAMMAR

After you have written your essay, it is important for you to review the grammar in your response.

> NOTE: For a review of grammar, see APPENDIX C.

Look at the following sentence from an essay on the effects of television.

> Television certainly *has changing* society in *very* big way.

In this sentence, the past participle rather than the present participle *changing* should be used after the helping verb *has*; to correct this error, you can change *changing* to *changed*. The article *a* also needs to be added because the countable singular noun *way* requires an article; to correct this error, you can change *very* to *a very*.

The following chart outlines the key information you should remember about reviewing grammar.

REVIEWING GRAMMAR	
GRAMMAR	Check for errors in grammar in your response. Be sure to check for errors with nouns and pronouns, verbs, adjectives and adverbs, articles, and agreement.

WRITING EXERCISE 15: Correct the errors in grammar in the following passages. (The number in parentheses at the end of each paragraph indicates the number of errors in the paragraph.)

Paragraph

1   In my first semester at the university, I was overwhelm by the differences between university studies and high school studies. In high school, I had easily be able to finish the number of work that was assigned, and if on certain occasion I did not complete an assignment, the teacher quickly tells me to make up the work. The situation in my university classes were not at all like the situation in high school. *(6)*

2   I was tremendously surprising at the volume of work assigned in the university. Unlike high school courses, which perhaps covered a chapter in two week, university courses regular covered two or three chapters in one week and two or three other chapters in the next week. I have been able to keep up with the workload in high school, but it was difficult for me to finish all the reading in mine university classes even though I tried real hard to finish all of them. *(7)*

3   The role that the teacher took in motivating students to get work done were also very different in my university. In high school, if an assignment was unfinishing on a date that it was due, my teacher would immediate let me know that I had made really a mistake and needed to finish an assignment right away. In my university classes, however, professors did not inform regularly students to make sure that we were get work done on schedule. It was really easy to put off studying in the beginning of each semesters and really have to work hard later in the semester to catch up on my assignments. *(9)*

4   During my first year in the university, I had to set firm goal to get things done by myself instead of relying on others to watch over me and make sure that I have done what I was supposed to do. With so much assignments, this was quite a task difficult, but I now regular try to do my best because I dislike being very far behind. It seems that I have turn into quite a motivating student. *(7)*

WRITING REVIEW EXERCISE (Skills 9–15):

Read the question. On a piece of paper, take notes on the main points of a response. Then write your response.

> Some people show their emotions, while other people work hard to keep their emotions from showing. What are the advantages of each type of behavior? Which do you try to do?

Response Time: 20 minutes

WRITING POST-TEST

Writing

Section Directions

This section tests your ability to communicate in writing in an academic environment. There are two writing tasks.

In the first writing task, you will read a passage and listen to a lecture. Then you will answer a question using information from the passage and the lecture. In the second task, you will answer a question using your own background knowledge.

Integrated Writing Directions

For this task, you will read a passage about an academic topic. You have **3 minutes** to read the passage, and then the passage will disappear. Then you will hear a lecture about the same topic. You can take notes while you read and listen.

You will then write an answer to a question about the relationship between the reading passage and the lecture. Try to use information from the passage and the lecture to answer the question. You will **not** be asked for your personal opinion. You can see the reading passage again when you are ready to write. You can use your notes to help you. You have **20 minutes** to write your response.

A successful answer will usually be around 150 to 225 words. Try to show that you can write well and give complete, accurate information.

Remember that you can see the passage again when you write your response. As soon as the reading time ends, the lecture will begin.

Independent Writing Directions

In this task, you will write an essay that states, explains, and supports your opinion about an issue. You have **30 minutes** to plan, write, and revise your essay.

A successful essay will usually be at least 300 words. Try to show that you can write well by developing your ideas, organizing your essay, and using language accurately to express your ideas.

Question 1
Read the passage. On a piece of paper, take notes on the main points of the reading passage.

    According to the law of unintended consequences, actions of individuals, groups, or governments have effects, or "consequences" that are unexpected, or "unintended." These unexpected effects, or unintended consequences as they are called in academic literature, are effects that are not planned when an original action is taken, and the person or persons making the decision do not consider that these effects may result from the action taken.

    Unintended consequences may turn out to be positive or negative. Unintended consequences that are positive may result, for example, from a decision by a city council to ban cars from Main Street in the city. If, as a result of this decision, there is an unexpected effect that many citizens improve their health because they need to park their cars and walk on a regular basis to get to the businesses that line Main Street, then this is a positive effect. There can, however, also be negative consequences of this decision by the city council to ban cars on Main Street. If, as a result of this decision, citizens decide that it is too much trouble to get to the businesses on Main Street because they cannot take their cars there, then they might decide to go to businesses elsewhere because it is easier to get there. A loss in the number of customers visiting the businesses along Main Street would be a definitely negative effect of the decision by the city council that was absolutely not intended by the city council when the decision was made.

Listen to the passage. On a piece of paper, take notes on the main points of the listening passage.

Now answer the following question:

        How does the information in the listening passage add to the ideas
        presented in the reading passage?

Question 2

Read the question. On a piece of paper, take notes on the main points of a response. Then write your response.

> Do you agree or disagree with the following statement?
> *It is better to be safe than sorry.*
> Use reasons and examples to support your response.

Turn to pages 128–134 to *assess* the skills used in the test, *score* the test using the Writing Scoring Criteria, and *record* your results.

WRITING MINI-TEST 1

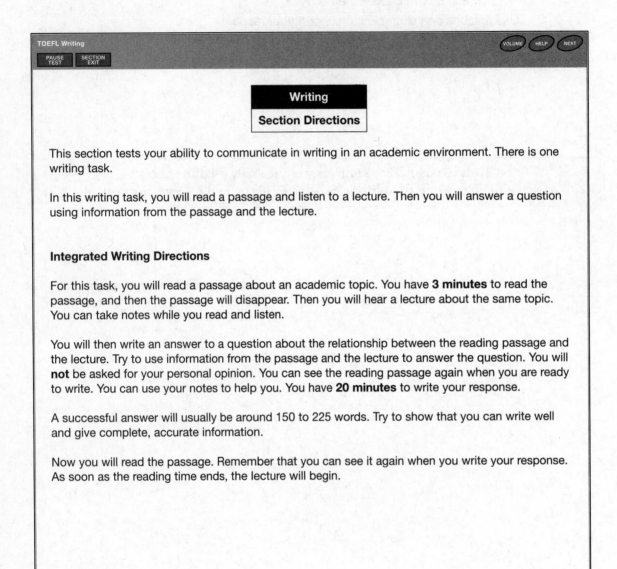

TOEFL Writing

PAUSE TEST | SECTION EXIT

VOLUME | HELP | NEXT

Writing
Section Directions

This section tests your ability to communicate in writing in an academic environment. There is one writing task.

In this writing task, you will read a passage and listen to a lecture. Then you will answer a question using information from the passage and the lecture.

Integrated Writing Directions

For this task, you will read a passage about an academic topic. You have **3 minutes** to read the passage, and then the passage will disappear. Then you will hear a lecture about the same topic. You can take notes while you read and listen.

You will then write an answer to a question about the relationship between the reading passage and the lecture. Try to use information from the passage and the lecture to answer the question. You will **not** be asked for your personal opinion. You can see the reading passage again when you are ready to write. You can use your notes to help you. You have **20 minutes** to write your response.

A successful answer will usually be around 150 to 225 words. Try to show that you can write well and give complete, accurate information.

Now you will read the passage. Remember that you can see it again when you write your response. As soon as the reading time ends, the lecture will begin.

Read the passage. On a piece of paper, take notes on the main points of the reading passage.

Reading Time: 3 minutes

Garlic, a member of the lily family with its distinctive odor and taste, has been used throughout recorded history because it was considered to have beneficial properties. The earliest known record of its use is in Sanskrit records from 3,000 B.C.

It was used as a medicine in Ancient Egypt, where it was used to cure twenty-two different ailments. It was also fed to the slaves who were building the pyramids because the Egyptians believed that, in addition to keeping the slaves healthy so that they could continue to work, garlic would make the slaves stronger so that they could work harder.

The ancient Greeks and Romans found even more uses for garlic than the Egyptians had. In addition to using garlic to cure illnesses, as the Egyptians had, the Greeks and Romans believed that garlic had magical powers, that it could ward off evil spells and curses. Garlic was also fed to soldiers because it was believed to make men more courageous.

Quite a few seafaring cultures have also used garlic because they believed that it was beneficial in helping sailors to endure long voyages. Homer used it on his odysseys, the Vikings always carried garlic on their long voyages in the northern seas, and Marco Polo left records showing that garlic was carried on his voyages to the Orient.

Finally, even as late as early in the twentieth century, it was believed that garlic could fight infections. Because of this belief, garlic juice was applied to soldiers' wounds in World War I to keep infection at bay and to prevent gangrene.

Listen to the passage. On a piece of paper, take notes on the main points of the listening passage.

Now answer the following question:

How does the information in the listening passage support the information presented in the reading passage?

Preparation Time: 1 minute
Response Time: 20 minutes

Turn to pages 128–134 to *assess* the skills used in the test, *score* the test using the Writing Scoring Criteria, and *record* your results.

WRITING MINI-TEST 2

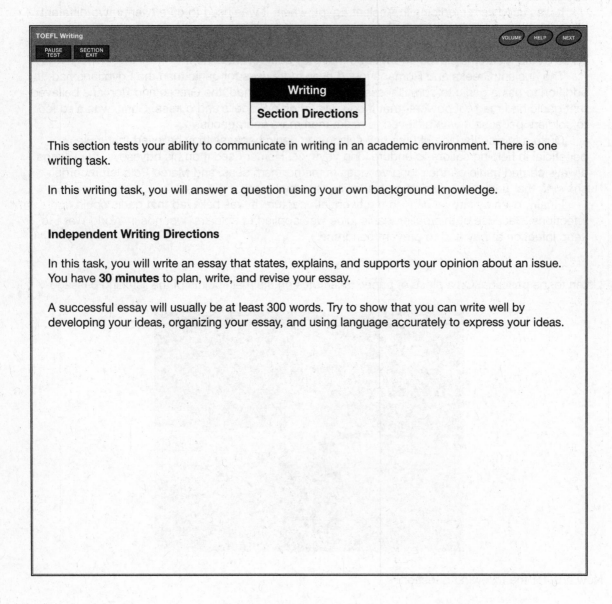

TOEFL Writing

PAUSE TEST | SECTION EXIT

VOLUME | HELP | NEXT

Writing
Section Directions

This section tests your ability to communicate in writing in an academic environment. There is one writing task.

In this writing task, you will answer a question using your own background knowledge.

Independent Writing Directions

In this task, you will write an essay that states, explains, and supports your opinion about an issue. You have **30 minutes** to plan, write, and revise your essay.

A successful essay will usually be at least 300 words. Try to show that you can write well by developing your ideas, organizing your essay, and using language accurately to express your ideas.

Read the question. On a piece of paper, take notes on the main points of a response. Then write your response.

What historical event in your country has had a major effect on your country? Give reasons and examples to support your response.

Response Time: 30 minutes

Turn to pages 128–134 to *assess* the skills used in the test, *score* the test using the Writing Scoring Criteria, and *record* your results.

WRITING MINI-TEST 3

TOEFL Writing

PAUSE TEST | SECTION EXIT

VOLUME | HELP | NEXT

Writing
Section Directions

This section tests your ability to communicate in writing in an academic environment. There is one writing task.

In this writing task, you will read a passage and listen to a lecture. Then you will answer a question using information from the passage and the lecture.

Integrated Writing Directions

For this task, you will read a passage about an academic topic. You have **3 minutes** to read the passage, and then the passage will disappear. Then you will hear a lecture about the same topic. You can take notes while you read and listen.

You will then write an answer to a question about the relationship between the reading passage and the lecture. Try to use information from the passage and the lecture to answer the question. You will **not** be asked for your personal opinion. You can see the reading passage again when you are ready to write. You can use your notes to help you. You have **20 minutes** to write your response.

A successful answer will usually be around 150 to 225 words. Try to show that you can write well and give complete, accurate information.

Now you will read the passage. Remember that you can see it again when you write your response. As soon as the reading time ends, the lecture will begin.

Read the passage. On a piece of paper, take notes on the main points of the reading passage.

Reading Time: 3 minutes

Frederick Winslow Taylor, author of *The Principles of Scientific Management* (1911), was a leading proponent of the scientific management movement in the early twentieth century, a movement dedicated to improving the speed and efficiency of workers on factory floors. In order to institute the principles of scientific management in factories, managers would first conduct thorough time-and-motion studies in which they sent out time-and-motion inspectors to workstations with stopwatches and rulers to time and measure the movements each factory worker was making in doing his or her job. The purpose of these studies was to identify wasted motion and energy in order to improve efficiency and thereby improve productivity and factory profits.

According to Taylor's principles, scientific managers could use the results of extensive time-and-motion studies to institute changes in their factories in order to make the factories more efficient. One major type of change that could be instituted as a result of time-and-motion studies was that the jobs of lower-skilled workers could be reorganized. Lower-skilled workers could also be instructed in the most efficient way of doing their jobs, instructed in how to stand and where to look, and instructed in how to move their bodies. Another major type of change was that higher-skilled and more highly paid workers could be replaced with lower-skilled and lower-paid workers. If the jobs of the more highly skilled workers could be broken down into more manageable tasks, then lower-skilled workers could more easily be brought in to replace various components of a higher-skilled worker's job. Factory management hoped that, by instituting these kinds of changes as a result of scientific time-and-motion studies, there could be greatly improved efficiency and lower costs, and therefore much greater profits, in the factories.

Listen to the passage. On a piece of paper, take notes on the main points of the listening passage.

Now answer the following question:

How do the ideas in the listening passage cast doubt on the ideas in the reading passage?

Preparation Time: 1 minute
Response Time: 20 minutes

Turn to pages 128–134 to *assess* the skills used in the test, *score* the test using the Writing Scoring Criteria, and *record* your results.

WRITING MINI-TEST 4

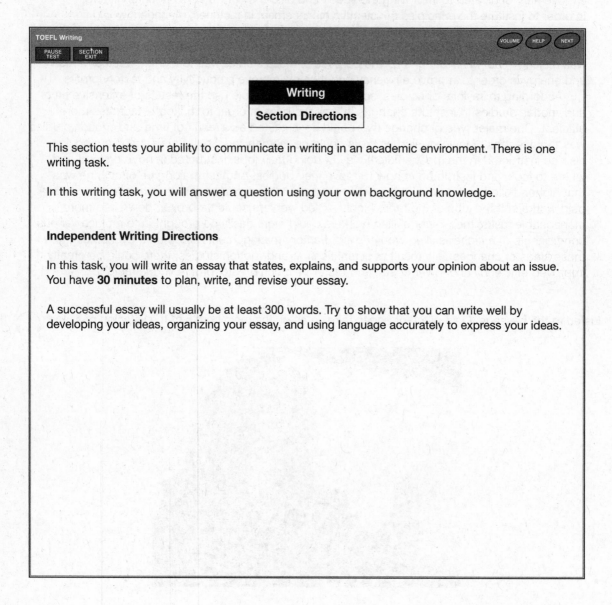

PAUSE TEST | SECTION EXIT

VOLUME | HELP | NEXT

Writing

Section Directions

This section tests your ability to communicate in writing in an academic environment. There is one writing task.

In this writing task, you will answer a question using your own background knowledge.

Independent Writing Directions

In this task, you will write an essay that states, explains, and supports your opinion about an issue. You have **30 minutes** to plan, write, and revise your essay.

A successful essay will usually be at least 300 words. Try to show that you can write well by developing your ideas, organizing your essay, and using language accurately to express your ideas.

Read the question. On a piece of paper, take notes on the main points of a response. Then write your response.

> Some people prefer to take a position in a company and work for the company. Other people think it is better to go into business for themselves. Which do you think is better? Give reasons and examples to support your response.

Response Time: 30 minutes

Turn to pages 128–134 to *assess* the skills used in the test,
score the test using the Writing Scoring Criteria, and *record* your results.

WRITING MINI-TEST 5

This section tests your ability to communicate in writing in an academic environment. There is one writing task.

In this writing task, you will read a passage and listen to a lecture. Then you will answer a question using information from the passage and the lecture.

Integrated Writing Directions

For this task, you will read a passage about an academic topic. You have **3 minutes** to read the passage, and then the passage will disappear. Then you will hear a lecture about the same topic. You can take notes while you read and listen.

You will then write an answer to a question about the relationship between the reading passage and the lecture. Try to use information from the passage and the lecture to answer the question. You will **not** be asked for your personal opinion. You can see the reading passage again when you are ready to write. You can use your notes to help you. You have **20 minutes** to write your response.

A successful answer will usually be around 150 to 225 words. Try to show that you can write well and give complete, accurate information.

Now you will read the passage. Remember that you can see it again when you write your response. As soon as the reading time ends, the lecture will begin.

Read the passage. On a piece of paper, take notes on the main points of the reading passage.

Reading Time: 3 minutes

Joseph Heller's *Catch-22* (1961) is one of the most acclaimed novels of the twentieth century. It is a black comedy about life in the military during World War II. It features bombardier John Yossarian, who is trying to survive the military's inexhaustible supply of bureaucracy and who is frantically trying to do anything to avoid killing and being killed. Heller was able to use his own experiences in the Air Force during World War II to create this character and the novel.

Even though *Catch-22* eventually became known as a great novel, it was not originally considered one. When it was first published in 1961, the reviews were tepid and the sales were lackluster. It was not well received at this point at least in part because it presented such a cowardly protagonist at a time when World War II veterans were being lauded for their selfless courage.

Within a few years of the release of the book, as an unpopular war in Southeast Asia was heating up, Heller's *Catch-22* found a new audience eager to enjoy the exploits of Heller's war-averse protagonist. It was within the framework of this era that *Catch-22* was newly discovered, newly examined, and newly credited as one of the century's best novels.

Listen to the passage. On a piece of paper, take notes on the main points of the listening passage.

Now answer the following question:

How does the information in the listening passage add to the ideas presented in the reading passage?

Preparation Time: 1 minute
Response Time: 20 minutes

Turn to pages 128–134 to *assess* the skills used in the test,
score the test using the Writing Scoring Criteria, and *record* your results.

WRITING MINI-TEST 6

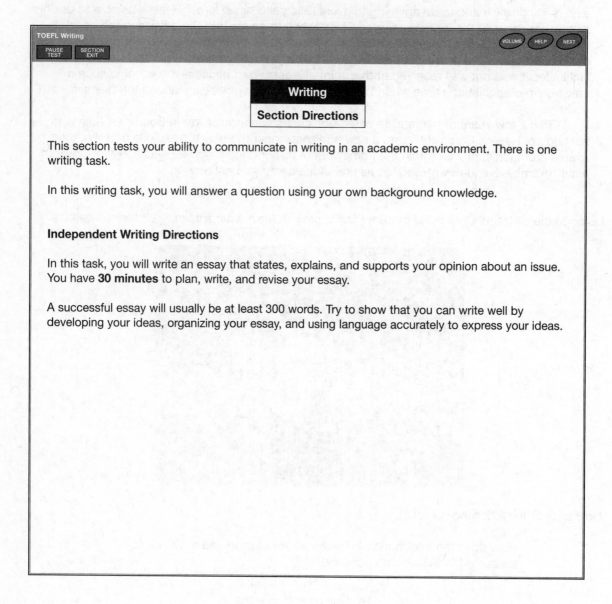

TOEFL Writing

PAUSE TEST SECTION EXIT

VOLUME HELP NEXT

Writing

Section Directions

This section tests your ability to communicate in writing in an academic environment. There is one writing task.

In this writing task, you will answer a question using your own background knowledge.

Independent Writing Directions

In this task, you will write an essay that states, explains, and supports your opinion about an issue. You have **30 minutes** to plan, write, and revise your essay.

A successful essay will usually be at least 300 words. Try to show that you can write well by developing your ideas, organizing your essay, and using language accurately to express your ideas.

Read the question. On a piece of paper, take notes on the main points of a response. Then write your response.

Traveling to a different country can be both exciting and frustrating at the same time. What are the most important pieces of advice that you would give visitors coming to your country? Give reasons and details to support your response.

Response Time: 30 minutes

Turn to pages 128–134 to *assess* the skills used in the test, *score* the test using the Writing Scoring Criteria, and *record* your results.

WRITING MINI-TEST 7

PAUSE TEST SECTION EXIT

VOLUME HELP NEXT

Writing
Section Directions

This section tests your ability to communicate in writing in an academic environment. There is one writing task.

In this writing task, you will read a passage and listen to a lecture. Then you will answer a question using information from the passage and the lecture.

Integrated Writing Directions

For this task, you will read a passage about an academic topic. You have **3 minutes** to read the passage, and then the passage will disappear. Then you will hear a lecture about the same topic. You can take notes while you read and listen.

You will then write an answer to a question about the relationship between the reading passage and the lecture. Try to use information from the passage and the lecture to answer the question. You will **not** be asked for your personal opinion. You can see the reading passage again when you are ready to write. You can use your notes to help you. You have **20 minutes** to write your response.

A successful answer will usually be around 150 to 225 words. Try to show that you can write well and give complete, accurate information.

Now you will read the passage. Remember that you can see it again when you write your response. As soon as the reading time ends, the lecture will begin.

Read the passage. On a piece of paper, take notes on the main points of the reading passage.

Reading Time: 3 minutes

In simple terms, a supernova is a star that explodes. During a supernova, a star brightens considerably over a period of about a week and then starts to fade slowly, over a period of a few months or a year or two before it disappears completely.

One kind of supernova is called a Type I supernova. This kind of supernova occurs in a double star system in which one of the stars has become a white dwarf. A double star system, or a binary star, is a pair of stars that are held together by the force of gravity and orbit around each other; a white dwarf is a formerly medium-sized star in the last stages of its life, a star that has run out of fuel and has collapsed into a small, dense star that is smaller than our planet. A Type I supernova occurs only in this very specific situation, when a white dwarf is part of a double star system.

A Type I supernova occurs in a double star system in a situation when a white star's companion star has grown too big. The companion star is always growing, and the white dwarf's companion star will continue to grow in size until its proximity to the white dwarf causes its growth to halt. When the companion star can grow no further, material from the companion star flows from the companion star to the white dwarf. When the white dwarf reaches a certain critical mass, a mass equal to approximately 1.4 times the mass of the Sun, the white dwarf explodes catastrophically in a supernova event.

Only two Type I supernovae have been visible to the naked eye in recorded history, one in 1572 and the other in 1604. Since then, numerous other Type I supernovae have been observed using the telescope, which was invented by Gallileo in 1610.

Listen to the passage. On a piece of paper, take notes on the main points of the listening passage.

Now answer the following question:

How does the information in the reading passage contrast with the information in the listening passage?

Preparation Time: 1 minute
Response Time: 20 minutes

Turn to pages 128–134 to *assess* the skills used in the test,
score the test using the Writing Scoring Criteria, and *record* your results.

WRITING MINI-TEST 8

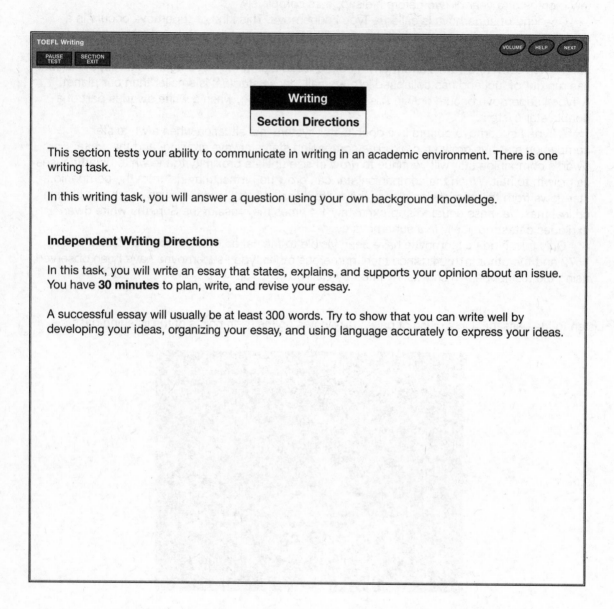

PAUSE TEST   SECTION EXIT

VOLUME   HELP   NEXT

Writing
Section Directions

This section tests your ability to communicate in writing in an academic environment. There is one writing task.

In this writing task, you will answer a question using your own background knowledge.

Independent Writing Directions

In this task, you will write an essay that states, explains, and supports your opinion about an issue. You have **30 minutes** to plan, write, and revise your essay.

A successful essay will usually be at least 300 words. Try to show that you can write well by developing your ideas, organizing your essay, and using language accurately to express your ideas.

Read the question. On a piece of paper, take notes on the main points of a response. Then write your response.

Do you agree or disagree with the following statement?

I think there is too much violence in movies.

Give specific reasons and examples to support your response.

Response Time: 30 minutes

Turn to pages 128–134 to *assess* the skills used in the test,
score the test using the Writing Scoring Criteria, and *record* your results.

WRITING COMPLETE TEST 1

Writing
Section Directions

This section tests your ability to communicate in writing in an academic environment. There are two writing tasks.

In the first writing task, you will read a passage and listen to a lecture. Then you will answer a question using information from the passage and the lecture. In the second task, you will answer a question using your own background knowledge.

Integrated Writing Directions

For this task, you will read a passage about an academic topic. You have **3 minutes** to read the passage, and then the passage will disappear. Then you will hear a lecture about the same topic. You can take notes while you read and listen.

You will then write an answer to a question about the relationship between the reading passage and the lecture. Try to use information from the passage and the lecture to answer the question. You will **not** be asked for your personal opinion. You can see the reading passage again when you are ready to write. You can use your notes to help you. You have **20 minutes** to write your response.

A successful answer will usually be around 150 to 225 words. Try to show that you can write well and give complete, accurate information.

Remember that you can see the passage again when you write your response. As soon as the reading time ends, the lecture will begin.

Independent Writing Directions

In this task, you will write an essay that states, explains, and supports your opinion about an issue. You have **30 minutes** to plan, write, and revise your essay.

A successful essay will usually be at least 300 words. Try to show that you can write well by developing your ideas, organizing your essay, and using language accurately to express your ideas.

Question 1

Read the passage. On a piece of paper, take notes on the main points of the reading passage.

Reading Time: 3 minutes

Originally named after the Roman goddess of love, the planet Venus also used to be known as the Morning Star and the Evening Star because it shines so brightly that it is visible on Earth even when the Sun is only partially visible in the morning and the evening.

Why does Venus shine so brightly? One reason is certainly because Venus is so close to Earth; it is, in fact, the closest planet to Earth. However, its proximity to Earth is not the only reason that Venus appears to shine so brightly. Another reason that Venus shines so brightly is that it is covered in thick white clouds that reflect sunlight off of them.

For quite some time, all that we have been able to see of Venus is the thick clouds that surround it, and little else was known of the planet itself. Dozens of space probes were sent to Venus in the last part of the twentieth century, and most of them were destroyed before they were able to send back information about Venus's surface. One probe, however, did manage to transmit some messages before it, too, failed.

From this one partially successful probe, numerous amazing facts about Venus have been learned. The thick clouds that cover Venus, for example, are made of sulfuric acid rather than oxygen, and these thick clouds never part to let any sunshine in at all. Most amazingly, the temperature on Venus is extremely hot, somewhere around 900 degrees Fahrenheit.

Listen to the passage. On a piece of paper, take notes on the main points of the listening passage.

Now answer the following question:

How does the information in the listening passage add to the information presented in the reading passage?

Preparation Time: 1 minute
Response Time: 20 minutes

Question 2

Read the question. On a piece of paper, take notes on the main points of a response. Then write your response.

> Many families have important traditions that family members share. What is one of your family's important traditions? Use specific reasons and details to support your response.

Response Time: 30 minutes

Turn to pages 128–134 to *assess* the skills used in the test,
score the test using the Writing Scoring Criteria, and *record* your results.

WRITING COMPLETE TEST 2

This section tests your ability to communicate in writing in an academic environment. There are two writing tasks.

In the first writing task, you will read a passage and listen to a lecture. Then you will answer a question using information from the passage and the lecture. In the second task, you will answer a question using your own background knowledge.

Integrated Writing Directions

For this task, you will read a passage about an academic topic. You have **3 minutes** to read the passage, and then the passage will disappear. Then you will hear a lecture about the same topic. You can take notes while you read and listen.

You will then write an answer to a question about the relationship between the reading passage and the lecture. Try to use information from the passage and the lecture to answer the question. You will **not** be asked for your personal opinion. You can see the reading passage again when you are ready to write. You can use your notes to help you. You have **20 minutes** to write your response.

A successful answer will usually be around 150 to 225 words. Try to show that you can write well and give complete, accurate information.

Remember that you can see the passage again when you write your response. As soon as the reading time ends, the lecture will begin.

Independent Writing Directions

In this task, you will write an essay that states, explains, and supports your opinion about an issue. You have **30 minutes** to plan, write, and revise your essay.

A successful essay will usually be at least 300 words. Try to show that you can write well by developing your ideas, organizing your essay, and using language accurately to express your ideas.

Question 1

Read the passage. On a piece of paper, take notes on the main points of the reading passage.

Reading Time: 3 minutes

Hamilton School District had a serious problem in that an unacceptably high number of students were dropping out before graduating from high school. The district had come to the conclusion that much of the problem of a high drop-out rate was due to widespread social promotion. Social promotion occurs when students who have not mastered required material at a particular level are still promoted to the next level. The district came up with a solution intended to combat the problem of social promotion, thereby also dealing with the high drop-out rate. The solution the school district came up with was to test students at the end of the school year to determine if they were ready to move on to the next grade level. It was decided that it was infeasible to test all students at the end of each school year. Instead, it was decided that a more feasible solution was to test all students only at the end of the sixth grade to determine whether or not they were ready for junior high school.

The district had high hopes for the program. One outcome that it expected from the program was that social promotion would end. The fact that students had to be tested at the end of the sixth grade would show teachers that there was no point in socially promoting unprepared students in the early grades. Another outcome that the district expected was that more students would be better prepared in junior high school and high school. After all, if students had to pass a test to move from sixth grade into junior high school, then they would have to be prepared. A final expected outcome was that more students would graduate from high school. If students were better prepared for junior high school and high school, then it seemed natural that more students would graduate.

Listen to the passage. On a piece of paper, take notes on the main points of the listening passage.

Now answer the following question:

How do the ideas in the listening passage challenge the ideas in the reading passage?

Preparation Time: 1 minute
Response Time: 20 minutes

Question 2

Read the question. On a piece of paper, take notes on the main points of a response. Then write your response.

What are the characteristics of a good leader? Give reasons and examples to support your response.

Response Time: 30 minutes

Turn to pages 128–134 to *assess* the skills used in the test,
score the test using the Writing Scoring Criteria, and *record* your results.

APPENDIX A

COHESION

It is important when you are producing material on the TOEFL iBT that you use a variety of methods of creating **cohesion**.[1] You should be sure that you know how to use repeated and rephrased key ideas, pronouns and determiners, and transition expressions to create cohesion.

Appendix A1: USE REPEATED AND REPHRASED KEY IDEAS

One way to make your written and spoken English more cohesive is to use repeated and rephrased key ideas. Look at the following example of repeated and rephrased key ideas used for cohesion.

Example

I think that the most important characteristic in a friend is honesty. If someone is a friend, then he or she must be *honest*. I can trust someone only if he or she is truthful. If a friend of mine does not tell me the *truth*, then he or she can no longer be considered a friend.

In this example, the key idea *honesty* is repeated as *honest* and rephrased as *truthful* and *truth* to make the passage cohesive.

The following chart outlines the key information that you should remember about using repeated key ideas to make your written and spoken English more cohesive.

USING REPEATED AND REPHRASED KEY IDEAS FOR COHESION

1. It is important to make your written and spoken English as cohesive as possible.
2. One way to make your written and spoken English more cohesive is to use repeated key ideas.
3. Another way to make your written and spoken English more cohesive is to use rephrased key ideas.
4. Repeated and rephrased key ideas are not the only way to make your written and spoken English cohesive. You should use a variety of ways to make your English cohesive.

---

[1] **Cohesion** is a characteristic of language in which ideas flow or attach together smoothly.

APPENDIX EXERCISE A1: Fill in the blanks in each pair of sentences with one of the words from the box above the pairs of sentences to make the sentences cohesive. You should use each answer one time only.

chance	competitor	energy	outcome	pleases	shocked	speaks

1. I am happy you have the opportunity to go there. It _____ me that you have been given such a _____.

2. She is quite a dynamic speaker. She always _____ with a great amount of _____.

3. The results of the competition were entirely unexpected. The _____ was _____ by the _____.

acts	brief	determined	positive	problems	remarks	resolved

4. The lawyer made a short statement. His _____ were quite _____.

5. The problems are not insurmountable. The _____ can be _____.

6. If you look at his actions in a negative way, you might say that he is stubborn. Conversely, if you look at the way he _____ in a _____ way, you might say that he is _____.

answers	complex	eventually	explanation	finish	indicated	succinct

7. She said that she would get it done sometime. She _____ that she would _____ it _____.

8. I do not want you to ramble on and on in your responses. Your _____ should be _____.

9. You have explained this in an overly simplistic way. You really need a more _____ _____.

animated	appreciates	concept	discussions	episode	involved	novel	reasons

10. Your idea is quite innovative. It is a _____ _____.

11. This professor seems to welcome lively debate. He _____ _____ _____.

12. Can you explain why you took part in this incident? Can you give me your _____ for being _____ in this _____?

Appendix A2: USE PRONOUNS AND DETERMINERS

Another way to make your written and spoken English more cohesive is to use **pronouns**[2] and **determiners**[3] to refer back to previous ideas. Some pronouns and determiners that can be used for cohesion are listed in the following table.

PRONOUNS					DETERMINERS	
SUBJECT	OBJECT	POSSESSIVE	REFLEXIVE	DEMONSTRATIVE	POSSESSIVE	DEMONSTRATIVE
I	me	mine	myself	this	my	this
you	you	yours	yourself	that	your	that
he	him	his	himself	these	his	these
she	her	hers	herself	those	her	those
it	it		itself		its	
we	us	ours	ourselves		our	
you	you	yours	yourselves		your	
they	them	theirs	themselves		their	

Look at the following example showing pronouns and determiners used for cohesion.

> **Example**
>
> A certain student worked very hard on a project. *He* did all of the work on *it* by *himself,* and *his* professor was very pleased with *this* work.

In this example, the pronoun *He* refers to the noun *student,* the pronoun *it* refers to the noun *project,* the pronoun *himself* refers to the noun *student,* the determiner *his* refers to the noun *student,* and the determiner *this* refers to the noun *work.* These pronouns and determiners help to make the passage cohesive.

The following chart outlines the key information that you should remember about using pronouns and determiners to make your written and spoken English more cohesive.

> **USING PRONOUNS AND DETERMINERS FOR COHESION**
>
> 1. It is important to make your written and spoken English as cohesive as possible.
> 2. One way to make your written and spoken English more cohesive is to use pronouns to refer back to previous ideas.
> 3. Another way to make your written and spoken English more cohesive is to use determiners to refer back to previous ideas.
> 4. Pronouns and determiners are not the only way to make your written and spoken English cohesive. You should use a variety of ways to make your English cohesive.

---

[2] **Pronouns** are words that take the place of nouns.
[3] **Determiners** are words that accompany nouns to identify the nouns.

APPENDIX EXERCISE A2: Fill in each blank with one of the pronouns or determiners from the box above the passage to make the passage cohesive. You should use each answer one time only.

her	herself	she	them	this	this

1. A researcher has been conducting a study on the causes of a certain disease. She has been conducting _____ study by _____. Up to now, _____ has determined several possible causes of the disease and has decided to focus on the most promising of _____. Though _____ research has not yet yielded a conclusive result, the researcher hopes _____ will happen soon.

it	mine	our	our	ourselves	ourselves	this	we	your

2. You and I have _____ work cut out for _____. You have to finish _____ part of the project, and I have to finish _____. Then when we have each finished _____ own parts of the project, _____ can get together to finish _____. We have to take it upon _____ to get _____ project done.

their	them	themselves	themselves	these	they	they

3. Some students have a huge assignment to complete by Friday. However, _____ students have procrastinated for quite some time, and now _____ are in a bit of a fix, so _____ only hope of finishing the assignment on time is for _____ to stay up all night for the next two nights to get it done. The students have gotten _____ into this situation, and now _____ will have to work very hard to get _____ out of it.

he	he	he	him	himself	his	his	it	this

4. A particular student is regretting that he signed up for a particular course. Unfortunately, _____ signed up for _____ course because _____ thought that _____ could be quite interesting. It did not take long for _____ to figure out that _____ reasoning had been rather faulty. He told _____ that _____ needed to be more careful in _____ decision-making in the future.

Appendix A3: USE TRANSITION EXPRESSIONS

A third way to make your written and spoken English more cohesive is to use transition expressions to show how ideas are related. Some transition expressions that can be used for cohesion are listed in the following table.

TRANSITION EXPRESSIONS			
EXPRESSION	MEANING	EXPRESSION	MEANING
therefore *as a result* *thus* *consequently*	result follows result follows result follows result follows	*in addition* *moreover* *furthermore*	more information follows more information follows more information follows
for example *for instance*	example follows example follows	*in contrast* *on the other hand* *nevertheless* *nonetheless* *however*	opposite information follows opposite information follows unexpected information follows unexpected information follows opposite or unexpected information follows
in conclusion *in summary*	conclusion follows conclusion follows		
in fact *indeed*	emphasis follows emphasis follows	*fortunately* *surprisingly* *interestingly*	something lucky follows something unexpected follows something unexpected follows

Look at the following example showing transition expressions used for cohesion.

> **Example**
>
> A group of students really wanted a certain program to be added to the university curriculum. The students presented their request to the university; *in addition,* they got hundreds of signatures on a petition. *Nonetheless,* their request was denied.

In this example, the transitions *in addition* and *Nonetheless* are used to make the passage cohesive.

The following chart outlines the key information that you should remember about using transition expressions to make your written and spoken English more cohesive.

> **USING TRANSITION EXPRESSIONS FOR COHESION**
>
> 1. It is important to make your written and spoken English as cohesive as possible.
> 2. One way to make your written and spoken English more cohesive is to use transition expressions to show how ideas are related.
> 3. Transition expressions are not the only way to make your written and spoken English cohesive. You should use a variety of ways to make your English cohesive.

APPENDIX EXERCISE A3: Fill in each blank with one of the transition expressions from the box above the passage to make the passage cohesive. You should use each answer one time only.

For instance	Fortunately	Furthermore	However	In fact

1. I certainly thought he would do a good job. _____, he failed miserably.

2. There are many ways to make a good impression on your boss. _____, one way is to come to work on time.

3. You should always show up for work on time. _____, you should never leave work early.

4. I can argue that you need to spend more time on this job. _____, you should spend several hours on it.

5. He tried recently to get that job. _____, that job is now his.

in contrast	in summary	moreover	nonetheless	therefore

6. Freshmen are taking the introductory course; juniors, _____, are taking the advanced course.

7. Freshmen have already studied biology; _____, they must still take the introductory biology course.

8. A certain course is required for freshmen; all freshmen, _____, must take the course.

9. Freshmen must take three lecture courses; _____, they must take one laboratory course.

10. Juniors must take three lecture courses and three laboratory courses; _____, they will be very busy.

as a result	for example	in conclusion	on the other hand	surprisingly

11. One student studied really hard for the exam; _____, she failed the exam.

12. A few students did quite well on the exam; the rest, _____, did quite poorly.

13. There were a few high grades on the exam. One student, _____, had 99% correct.

14. Some students did not prepare for the exam; _____, they did not do so well.

15. The students who studied hard did well on the exam, and those who did not study hard did poorly; _____, one can say that the exam grades depended on preparation.

| consequently | in addition | indeed | interestingly | nevertheless |

16. Tickets are required for the concert; _____, anyone who wants to go to the concert must purchase a ticket.

17. A sonata will be performed at the concert; _____, a concerto will be performed.

18. One students does not like classical music; _____, her friends have talked her into going.

19. There will be a guest performer at the concert; _____, the guest performer is someone quite famous.

20. The audience truly appreciated the performance; _____, the audience thought the performance was wonderful.

APPENDIX REVIEW EXERCISE (A1–A3): Put parentheses around the cohesive devices in the following passages. Label each as (A) a repeated or rephrased key idea, (B) a pronoun or determiner, or (C) a transition expression.

1. The young man gave an explanation for his unusual behavior. (It) was that (he) had been afraid. (His) (fear) had caused him to (act) this way.

2. The board has indicated that it is now in accord on the key point of the bill. However, agreement on this main point was not easy for the board to reach.

3. The professor discussed several important concepts in the lecture. The focus of her lecture was the development of these concepts.

4. One member of the group was opposed to the plan. He objected vociferously. Nonetheless, the plan was implemented immediately.

5. Assignments must be turned in on time. Absolutely no late assignments will be accepted. In fact, any assignment that is not submitted on time will receive a grade of zero.

6. An account of the incident appeared in the newspaper. Unfortunately, many of the details in this account were not accurate. The newspaper needs to print a retraction to correct these inaccuracies.

7. You must decide whether to write a thesis or to take a comprehensive exam, and you must make this decision yourself. Choosing between a thesis and a comprehensive exam is a major decision.

8. Even in the beginning, all the members of the group worked very hard on the project. Indeed, from the outset, a huge amount of effort was invested in the project. Not surprisingly, their effort was not wasted; they were rewarded with a high grade on the project.

9. The professor gave an assignment in class today. However, the students are confused about what the assignment actually is. The professor spoke for quite some time about the assignment, but he said a number of contradictory things. These contradictory things are what caused the students to be confused.

10. A number of major corporations are sending representatives to campus this week to interview students who are seeking jobs in these corporations. Any students wishing to have interviews should sign up in the campus placement office. The corporate representatives will be on campus for only a short time, and the number of interviews is limited. Thus, it is important to sign up for interviews immediately.

APPENDIX B
SENTENCE STRUCTURE _____

It is important when you are producing material on the TOEFL iBT that you use a variety of correct sentence structures. You should be sure that you know how to use simple sentences, compound sentences, and complex sentences.

Appendix B1: USE CORRECT SIMPLE SENTENCES

A simple sentence is a sentence that has only one **clause**.[4] Two types of sentence structure errors are common in sentences with only one clause: (1) the clause can be missing a subject or a verb, and (2) the clause can be introduced by a subordinate adverb clause connector.

The first type of incorrect simple sentence is a sentence that is missing a subject or a verb. (Note that an asterisk is used to indicate that a sentence contains an error.)

Generally, <u>is</u> important to fill out the form completely.*
VERB

The <u>ideas</u> for the construction of the project.*
SUBJECT

The first sentence is incorrect because it has the verb *is* but is missing a subject. The second sentence is incorrect because it has a subject *ideas* but is missing a verb.

Another type of incorrect simple sentence is one that includes a subordinate adverb clause connector in front of the subject and the verb. The following chart lists common subordinate adverb clause connectors.

SUBORDINATE ADVERB CLAUSE CONNECTORS					
TIME	CAUSE	CONDITION	CONTRAST	MANNER	PLACE
after once as since as long as until as soon as when before whenever by the time while	as because inasmuch as now that since	if in case provided providing unless whether	although even though though while whereas	as in that	where wherever

Look at the following examples of incomplete sentences.

Because the <u>manager</u> of the company <u>instructed</u> me to do it.*
SUBJECT   VERB

Even though the <u>contest</u> <u>was run</u> in an unfair manner.*
SUBJECT VERB

The first sentence is incorrect because the subordinate adverb clause connector *Because* is in front of the subject *manager* and the verb *instructed*. The second sentence is incorrect because

_____

[4] A **clause** is a group of words that has both a subject and a verb.

the subordinate adverb clause connector *Even though* is in front of the subject *contest* and the verb *was run*.

The following chart outlines the key information that you should remember about using correct simple sentences.

USING CORRECT SIMPLE SENTENCES
1. A simple sentence is a sentence with one clause.
2. A simple sentence must have both a subject and a verb.
3. A simple sentence may not be introduced by a subordinate adverb clause connector.

APPENDIX EXERCISE B1: Underline the subjects once and the verbs twice. Put parentheses around the subordinate clause connectors. Then indicate if the sentences are correct (C) or incorrect (I).

_____ 1. The obvious reasons for the selection of the candidate.

_____ 2. When everyone in the room decided to leave.

_____ 3. I found the ideas rather unsettling.

_____ 4. Often discusses the advantages of the situation.

_____ 5. A preference for movies with lots of action.

_____ 6. Fortunately, the piece of paper with the crucial information was found.

_____ 7. As soon as the article appears in the newspaper.

_____ 8. Definitely is not proper to make that suggestion.

_____ 9. His agreement with me about the important issues.

_____ 10. It happened that way.

_____ 11. As no one else in the world would have made the same decision.

_____ 12. Without any hesitation made a decision not to return.

_____ 13. An agreement as to the amount to be paid has been reached.

_____ 14. A poem written on a piece of faded parchment.

_____ 15. Now that you have told me about your childhood.

_____ 16. We forgot.

_____ 17. To take the medicine at the right time to be the most effective.

_____ 18. If you think about the problem just a little more.

_____ 19. Unfortunately, the manager already made the decision.

_____ 20. Even though you gave me a gift for my birthday.

Appendix B2: USE CORRECT COMPOUND SENTENCES

A compound sentence is a sentence that has more than one **main clause**.[5] The main clauses in a compound sentence can be connected correctly with a coordinate conjunction (*and, but, or, so, yet*) and a comma (,) or with a semi-colon (;). Look at the following examples.

> Jack studies hard. He gets high grades.
>
> Jack studies hard, so he gets high grades.
>
> Jack studies hard; he gets high grades.

In the first example, the two main clauses *Jack studies hard* and *He gets high grades* are not combined into a compound sentence. In the second example, the two main clauses are combined into a compound sentence with the coordinate conjunction *so* and a comma. In the third example, the same two main clauses are combined into a compound sentence with a semi-colon.

It is possible to use adverb transitions in compound sentences. (See Appendix A3 for a list of transition expressions.) It is important to note that adverb transitions are not conjunctions, so either a semi-colon or a coordinate conjunction with a comma is needed.

Look at the following examples of sentences with adverb transitions.

> Jack studies hard. As a result, he gets high grades.
>
> Jack studies hard, and, as a result, he gets high grades.
>
> Jack studies hard; as a result, he gets high grades.

In the first example, the two main clauses *Jack studies hard* and *he gets high grades* are not combined into a compound sentence even though the adverb transition *As a result* is used. In the second example, the two main clauses are combined into a compound sentence with the coordinate conjunction *and* and a comma; the adverb transition *as a result* is included after the coordinate conjunction. In the third example, the same two main clauses are combined into a compound sentence with a semi-colon, and the adverb transition is set off from the second main clause with a comma.

The following chart outlines the key information that you should remember about using correct compound sentences.

USING CORRECT COMPOUND SENTENCES

1. A compound sentence is a sentence with more than one main clause.
2. The main clauses in a compound sentence may be joined with either a semi-colon (;) or a coordinate conjunction (*and, but, or, so, yet*) and a comma (,).
3. An adverb transition can be used in a compound sentence, but either a semi-colon or a coordinate conjunction and a comma is still needed.

---

[5] A **main clause** is an independent clause that has both a subject and a verb and is not introduced by a subordinate clause connector.

APPENDIX EXERCISE B2: Underline the subjects once and the verbs twice in the main clauses. Put parentheses around the punctuation, transitions, and connectors that join the main clauses. Then indicate if the sentences are correct (C) or incorrect (I).

_____ 1. The matter was really important(,) I could to decide too quickly.

_____ 2. The children broke the rules, but their parents did not find out.

_____ 3. She expected to graduate in the spring, however she did not graduate until fall.

_____ 4. My family moved a lot during my youth; as a result, I always had to make new friends.

_____ 5. I made a firm promise to my friend and I vowed to keep it.

_____ 6. Sam did not sign in before work, so he signed in afterwards.

_____ 7. The students waited in a long line to register. Finally, they got to the front of the line.

_____ 8. His parents advised him to think about it some more he did not take their advice.

_____ 9. My first job in the company was as a part-time worker, later I was given a full-time job.

_____ 10. Tom really wanted to be successful, yet he did not know how to accomplish this.

_____ 11. We must return the books to the library today, otherwise we will have to pay a fine.

_____ 12. She always tries not to get too angry. However, she sometimes loses her temper.

_____ 13. Therefore she has gotten a job, she can pay all of her bills.

_____ 14. She had the surgery recommended by her doctor; as a result, she is doing better now.

_____ 15. They left the money in a savings account, it began to collect some interest.

_____ 16. I wanted to get a high-paying job last summer; unfortunately, this was impossible.

_____ 17. I will have to study harder, or I will not be able to get a scholarship.

_____ 18. An accident happened at the corner, afterwards, the police came and wrote a report.

_____ 19. The plan has a number of advantages it also has a number of disadvantages.

_____ 20. The directions must be followed exactly; otherwise, the outcome will be very bad.

Appendix B3: USE CORRECT COMPLEX SENTENCES

A complex sentence is a sentence with one main clause and at least one **subordinate clause**.[6] Noun, adjective, and adverb clauses are all types of subordinate clauses. Each of the following sentences is a complex sentence because it contains a subordinate clause.

> I cannot believe (what he did).
> NOUN CLAUSE

> The runner (who finishes first) wins the trophy.
> ADJECTIVE CLAUSE

> I will return to the job (when I am able).
> ADVERB CLAUSE

The first complex sentence contains the subordinate noun clause *what he did*. The second complex sentence contains the subordinate adjective clause *who finishes first*. The final complex sentence contains the subordinate adverb clause *when I am able*.

A variety of errors with complex structures can occur in student writing, but two errors that occur with great frequency are (1) repeated subjects after adjective clauses, and (2) repeated subjects after noun clauses as subjects. To understand these two problems, you must recognize adjective and noun clauses. The following chart lists connectors that introduce adjective and noun clauses.

SUBORDINATE ADJECTIVE AND NOUN CLAUSE CONNECTORS				
ADJECTIVE CLAUSE CONNECTORS	NOUN CLAUSE CONNECTORS			
who	who	when	whichever	if
whom	whoever	whenever	why	that
which	what	where	how	
that	whatever	which	whether	

Look at the following examples of errors with adjective and noun clauses.

> A good <u>friend</u> (who lives down the street) <u>she</u>* <u>did</u> me a favor.
> SUBJECT   SUBJECT VERB

> (<u>What</u> my advisor told me yesterday) <u>it</u>* <u>was</u> very helpful.
> NOUN CLAUSE SUBJECT   SUBJECT VERB

The first sentence is incorrect because it contains an extra subject. The correct subject *friend* comes before the adjective clause *who lives down the street,* and an extra subject *she* comes after the adjective clause. To correct this sentence, you should omit the extra subject *she*. The second sentence is also incorrect because it contains an extra subject. *What my advisor told me yesterday* is a noun clause subject, and this noun clause subject is followed by the extra subject *it*. To correct this sentence, you should omit the extra subject *it*.

---

[6] A **subordinate clause** is a dependent clause that has both a subject and a verb and is introduced by a subordinate clause connector.

The following chart outlines the key information that you should remember about using correct complex sentences.

USING CORRECT COMPLEX SENTENCES

1. A complex sentence is a sentence with one main clause and one or more subordinate clauses.
2. Noun clauses, adjective clauses, and adverb clauses are subordinate clauses.
3. When a subject comes before an adjective clause, you should not add an extra subject after the adjective clause.
4. When a noun clause is used as a subject, you should not add an extra subject after the noun clause.

APPENDIX EXERCISE B3: Underline the subjects once and the verbs twice in the main clauses. Put parentheses around the subordinate noun and adjective clauses. Then indicate if the sentences are correct (C) or incorrect (I).

_____ 1. The reason (that) he took the money it was to pay the bills.

_____ 2. Why the man did something so terrible will never be known.

_____ 3. The ticket that I need to get onto the plane was not included in the packet.

_____ 4. What the lifeguard did it was quite heroic.

_____ 5. The day when I found out the news it was a good day.

_____ 6. The teacher whose advice I remember to this day was my sixth grade teacher.

_____ 7. Where we went on vacation it was such a gorgeous place.

_____ 8. That he really said those words it could not be refuted.

_____ 9. The man who helped me the most in my life he was my high school coach.

_____ 10. How the paper got finished on time remains unclear to me.

_____ 11. What caused the accident on the freeway it is still unknown.

_____ 12. The plans that we made for our trip were not carefully thought out.

_____ 13. The process by which the decisions were made it was very slow.

_____ 14. Whatever she gets is what she deserves.

_____ 15. The employee who has the information that you need is out of the office.

_____ 16. What he wrote in the letter it could not be taken back.

_____ 17. The officer who stopped me on the highway he gave me a ticket for speeding.

_____ 18. How he could believe something that is so incredible is beyond me.

_____ 19. The reason that I applied to the public school was that the tuition was lower.

_____ 20. Why they said what they said to the man who tried to help them it was not clear.

APPENDIX REVIEW EXERCISE (B1–B3): Correct the errors in the following passages.

1. I have two very personal reasons for coming to this conclusion. One of the reasons is related to my family relationships, the other is related to my finances.

2. A decision has been reached but the decision has not yet been announced. We must wait until four o'clock, that is when the decision will be announced.

3. What just happened this morning it was a complete shock to me. My math professor announced in class this morning that the exam that was scheduled for next Friday it would be given this morning. Unfortunately, I was not prepared for the exam this morning because did not expect the exam to be given then.

4. The department has announced that only two scholarships will be awarded and that more than a hundred applications for the scholarships have already been received. Nonetheless, I am still going to submit my application.

5. My family never really wanted to make so many moves, it had to do so. Because it was necessary for my father's career, so we moved almost every year.

6. I expect your papers to be very clearly organized; thus, you are required to turn in an outline before you complete your papers. Your outline should be turned in within two weeks; the final paper is not due for two months.

7. The university is considering implementing an increase in tuition for the coming year. The students believe that tuition should not be raised, however, the students will most likely not get what they want.

8. The details of the report are confidential, they will not be made public. If want to find out about the report, what you must do it is to file a petition to get hold of the report.

9. My dream house is one that would be in the mountains. It would be surrounded by trees and it would have a view of a gorgeous lake. Moreover, the only noises that could be heard they would be the sounds of birds singing.

10. You must develop your ideas thoroughly. If you make a statement, you should be sure to support that statement. You may use many kinds of ideas to support a statement. For example, you may use details, reasons, or examples.

APPENDIX C

ERROR CORRECTION

It is important when you are producing material on the TOEFL iBT that your English be grammatically correct. You should be sure that you know how to use subject/verb agreement, parallel structure, comparatives and superlatives, verb forms, verb uses, passives, nouns, pronouns, adjectives and adverbs, and articles correctly.

SUBJECT/VERB AGREEMENT

Subject/verb agreement is simple: if a subject is singular, then the verb that accompanies it must be singular, and if a subject is plural, then the verb that accompanies it must be plural.

> The <u>student</u> <u>takes</u> many exams.
>
> The <u>students</u> <u>take</u> many exams.

In the first example, the singular subject *student* requires the singular verb *takes*. In the second example, the plural subject *students* requires the plural verb *take*.

Although this might seem quite simple, there are some situations with subject/verb agreement that can be confusing. You should be careful of subject/verb agreement (1) after prepositional phrases, and (2) after expressions of quantity.

Appendix C1: MAKE VERBS AGREE AFTER PREPOSITIONAL PHRASES

Sometimes prepositional phrases can come between the subject and the verb. If the object of the preposition is singular and the subject is plural, or if the object of the preposition is plural and the subject is singular, there can be confusion in making the subject and verb agree. (Note that an asterisk indicates that there is an error.)

> The <u>key</u> (to the doors) <u>are</u>* in the drawer.
>
> The <u>keys</u> (to the door) <u>is</u>* in the drawer.

In the first example, you might think that *doors* is the subject because it comes directly in front of the verb *are*. However, *doors* is not the subject because it is the object of the preposition *to*. The subject is *key*, so the verb should be *is*. In the second example, you might think that *door* is the subject because it comes directly in front of the verb *is*. You should recognize in this example that *door* is not the subject because it is the object of the preposition *to*. Because the subject is *keys*, the verb should be *are*.

The following chart outlines the key information that you should understand about subject/verb agreement with prepositional phrases.

SUBJECT/VERB AGREEMENT WITH PREPOSITIONAL PHRASES
S *(prepositional phrase)* V
When a prepositional phrase comes between the subject and the verb, be sure that the verb agrees with the subject.

APPENDIX EXERCISE C1: Each of the following sentences has one or more prepositional phrases between the subject and the verb. Put parentheses around the prepositional phrases between the subject and verb. Underline the subjects once and the verbs twice. Then indicate if the sentences are correct (C) or incorrect (I).

___C___ 1. The forest <u>rangers</u> (in the eastern section) (of the park) <u><u>have spotted</u></u> a bear.

___I___ 2. The <u>flowers</u> (on the plum tree) (in the garden) <u><u>has started</u></u> to bloom.

(flowers . . . have started)

_____ 3. The cost of the books for all of his classes are quite high.

_____ 4. The reports prepared by the staff for the manager contain many graphs and charts.

_____ 5. The light from the candles on the end tables provide a soft glow to the room.

_____ 6. The ideas suggested at the meeting of the council was well received by most attendees.

_____ 7. The gemstones in the necklace worn by the actress were beautifully matched.

_____ 8. The speech on a variety of topics of great importance to the citizens are being broadcast this evening.

_____ 9. The new tires for the front of the car are being installed at this moment.

_____ 10. The exams scheduled for the last week of the semester is going to be comprehensive exams.

Appendix C2: MAKE VERBS AGREE AFTER EXPRESSIONS OF QUANTITY

A particular agreement problem occurs when the subject is an expression of quantity, such as *all, most,* or *some,* followed by the preposition *of.* In this situation, the subject (*all, most,* or *some*) can be singular or plural, depending on what follows the preposition *of.*

<u>All</u> (of the book) <u><u>was</u></u> interesting.

<u>All</u> (of the books) <u><u>were</u></u> interesting.

<u>All</u> (of the information) <u><u>was</u></u> interesting.

In the first example, the subject *All* refers to the singular noun *book.* In the second example, the subject *All* refers to the plural noun *books,* so the correct verb is the plural verb *were.* In the third example, the subject *All* refers to the uncountable noun *information,* so the correct verb is therefore the singular verb *was.*

The following chart outlines the key information that you should understand about subject/verb agreement after expressions of quantity.

SUBJECT/VERB AGREEMENT AFTER EXPRESSIONS OF QUANTITY
all most some   of the (OBJECT)   V half part
When an expression of quantity is the subject, the verb agrees with the object.

APPENDIX EXERCISE C2: Each of the following sentences has a quantity expression as the subject. Underline the subjects once and the verbs twice. Put parentheses around the objects that the verbs agree with. Then indicate if the sentences are correct (C) or incorrect (I).

__C__   1. <u>All</u> of his past (experience) <u>has contributed</u> to his present success.

__I__   2. <u>Most</u> of the (dishes) served at the banquet <u>was</u> quite spicy.
 (Most of the dishes served at the banquet were quite spicy.)

_____   3. Some of the details of the plan requires clarification.

_____   4. Half of the material needs to be completed this week.

_____   5. All of the homes on this block of town was flooded during the storm.

_____   6. Most of the children in the class has improved their reading scores tremendously.

_____   7. Some of the money from the inheritance has to be used to pay taxes.

_____   8. I bought a carton of eggs yesterday, but half of the eggs in the carton was broken.

_____   9. For her health to improve, all of the medicine has to be taken on schedule.

_____ 10. At the conference, most of the time allocated for speeches was actually devoted to discussion.

PARALLEL STRUCTURE

In good English, an attempt should be made to make the language as even and balanced as possible. This balance is called "parallel structure." You can achieve parallel structure by making the forms as similar as possible. The following is an example of a sentence that is not parallel.

> I like <u>to sing</u> and <u>dancing</u>.*

The problem in this sentence is not the expression *to sing,* and the problem is not the word *dancing.* The expression *to sing* is correct by itself, and the word *dancing* is correct by itself. Both of the following sentences are correct.

I like to sing.

I like dancing.

The problem in the incorrect example is that *to sing* and *dancing* are joined together in one sentence with *and*. They are different forms where it is possible to have similar forms; the example is therefore not parallel. It can be corrected in two different ways.

I like to sing and to dance.

I like singing and dancing.

Two issues in parallel structure that you should be familiar with are (1) the use of parallel structure with coordinate conjunctions, and (2) the use of parallel structure with paired conjunctions.

Appendix C3: USE PARALLEL STRUCTURE WITH COORDINATE CONJUNCTIONS

The job of coordinate conjunctions (*and, but, or, yet*) is to join together equal expressions. In other words, what is on one side of these words must be parallel to what is on the other side. These conjunctions can join nouns, or verbs, or adjectives, or phrases, or subordinate clauses; they just must join together two of the same thing. Look at the following examples.

She is not a teacher *but* a lawyer.

He studied hard *yet* failed the exam.

My boss is sincere, friendly, *and* nice.

The papers are on my desk *or* in the drawer.

I am here because I have to be *and* because I want to be.

In the first example, the coordinate conjunction *but* joins two nouns, *teacher* and *lawyer*. In the second example, the coordinate conjunction *yet* joins two verbs, *studied* and *failed*. In the third example, the coordinate conjunction *and* joins three adjectives, *sincere*, *friendly*, and *nice*. In the fourth example, the coordinate conjunction *or* joins two prepositional phrases, *on my desk* and *in the drawer*. In the last example, the coordinate conjunction *and* joins two clauses, *because I have to be* and *because I want to be*.

The following chart describes the use of parallel structures with coordinate conjunctions.

PARALLEL STRUCTURE WITH COORDINATE CONJUNCTIONS		
(same structure)	*and* *but* *or* *yet*	(same structure)
(same structure), (same structure),	*and* *but* *or* *yet*	(same structure)

APPENDIX EXERCISE C3: Each of the following sentences contains words or groups of words that should be parallel. Put parentheses around the word that indicates that the sentence should have parallel parts. Underline the parts that should be parallel. Then indicate if the sentences are correct (C) or incorrect (I).

__I__ 1. The movie <u>was really scary</u> (but) <u>was still quite pleasure</u>.
   (was still quite pleasurable)

__C__ 2. He said <u>that he was sorry</u> (and) <u>that he would make amends</u>.

_____ 3. The leader spoke of the need for idealism, integrity, and dedicate.

_____ 4. The ball player was not very tall yet was quite athlete.

_____ 5. To contact me, you may call on the phone, write a letter, or send a fax.

_____ 6. The course is offered in the spring semester but not in the fall semester.

_____ 7. For his job, he travels back and forth between Los Angeles and New York to pick up packages and delivers them.

_____ 8. He can work on the report in the library or studies at home.

_____ 9. The news report described the pain, anger, resentment, frustration, and disbelief in the aftermath of the accident.

_____ 10. She gave a well-rehearsed yet natural-sounding speech.

Appendix C4: USE PARALLEL STRUCTURE WITH PAIRED CONJUNCTIONS

The paired conjunctions *both . . . and, either . . . or, neither . . . nor,* and *not only . . . but also* require parallel structures. Look at the following examples.

> I know *both* <u>where you went</u> *and* <u>what you did</u>.
>
> *Either* <u>Mark</u> *or* <u>Sue</u> has the book.
>
> The tickets are *neither* <u>in my pocket</u> *nor* <u>in my purse</u>.
>
> He *not only* <u>works hard</u> *but also* <u>plays hard</u>.

In the first example, the paired conjunction *both . . . and* is followed by parallel clauses, *where you went* and *what you did*. In the second example, the paired conjunction *Either . . . or* is followed by parallel nouns, *Mark* and *Sue*. In the third example, the paired conjunction *neither . . . nor* is followed by parallel phrases, *in my pocket* and *in my purse*. In the last example, the paired conjunction *not only . . . but also* is followed by parallel verb phrases, *works hard* and *plays hard*.

The following chart describes the use of parallel structure with paired conjunctions.

PARALLEL STRUCTURE WITH PAIRED CONJUNCTIONS			
both either neither not only	(same structure)	and or nor but also	(same structure)

APPENDIX EXERCISE C4: Each of the following sentences contains words or groups of words that should be parallel. Put parentheses around the word or words that indicate that the sentence should have parallel parts. Underline the parts that should be parallel. Then indicate if the sentences are correct (C) or incorrect (I).

____I____ 1. He (not only) <u>plays football</u> (but also) <u>baseball</u>.
     (plays baseball)

____C____ 2. The children were (either) <u>praised</u> (or) <u>scolded</u> for their behavior.

_____ 3. There is food to eat both in the refrigerator and the freezer.

_____ 4. It has been decided to do neither what you prefer or what I prefer.

_____ 5. She not only misplaced her textbook but also couldn't find her notebook.

_____ 6. Either you can work on this committee or join a different one.

_____ 7. She was both challenged by and frustrated with her job.

_____ 8. Neither the manager nor any members of the staff are staying late today.

_____ 9. You can either register for three courses or for four courses.

_____ 10. Both the children as well as the baby-sitter fell asleep.

COMPARATIVES AND SUPERLATIVES

A comparative (formed with *-er* or *more*) shows how two items relate to each other, while a superlative (formed with *-est* or *most*) shows how one item relates to a group.

> My history class is much *harder* than my science class.
> My history class is much *more interesting* than my science class.
>
> My history class is *the hardest* of all my classes.
> My history class is *the most interesting* of all my classes.

In the first two examples, the comparatives *harder* and *more interesting* show how the history class relates to the science class. In the last two examples, the superlatives *the hardest* and *the most interesting* show how the history class relates to all of the classes.

Comparatives and superlatives are important in academic language. It is important for you to know how to do the following: (1) form the comparative and superlative correctly, and (2) use the comparative and superlative correctly.

Appendix C5: FORM COMPARATIVES AND SUPERLATIVES CORRECTLY

The comparative is formed with either *-er* or *more* and *than*. In the comparative, *-er* is used with shorter (one-syllable and some two-syllable) adjectives such as *tall*, and *more* is used with longer (some two-syllable and all three-or-more-syllable) adjectives such as *beautiful*.

> Rich is *taller than* Ron.
> Sally is *more beautiful than* Sharon.

The superlative is formed with *the*, either *-est* or *most*, and sometimes *in*, *of*, or a *that*-clause. In the superlative, *-est* is used with shorter adjectives such as *tall*, and *most* is used with longer adjectives such as *beautiful*.

> Rich is *the tallest* man *in* the room.
> Sally is *the most beautiful of* all the women in the room.
> The spider by the window is *the largest* one *that* I have ever seen.
> *The fastest* runner wins the race. (no *in*, *of*, or *that*)

The following chart outlines the possible forms of comparatives and superlatives.

FORMS OF COMPARATIVES AND SUPERLATIVES		
COMPARATIVE	short adjective + *-er* *more* + long adjective	*than*
SUPERLATIVE	*the* short adjective + *-est* *most* + long adjective	maybe *in*, *of*, *that*
Shorter adjectives are all one-syllable adjectives and some two-syllable adjectives. Longer adjectives are some two-syllable adjectives and all adjectives with three or more syllables.		

APPENDIX EXERCISE C5: Each of the following sentences contains a comparative or superlative. Put parentheses around the comparative or superlative. Then indicate if the sentences are correct (C) or incorrect (I).

__I__   1. This morning I heard (the unusualest) story in the news.
       (the most unusual)

__C__   2. This bicycle is (more expensive than) mine.

_____   3. Today she became the angriest that I have ever seen her.

_____   4. This classroom is the hotter than the one next door.

_____   5. The weather today is much more cloudier today than it was yesterday.

_____   6. This room houses the most ancient pieces of sculpture in the museum.

_____   7. The seats on this airline are wider than those on the airline that I took last week.

_____   8. The building where he works is the most tallest in town.

_____   9. This restaurant has most efficient service of all the restaurants I have visited.

_____ 10. This type of coffee is stronger and more flavorful than my regular coffee.

Appendix C6: USE COMPARATIVES AND SUPERLATIVES CORRECTLY

The comparative and superlative have different uses, and it is important to understand these differences. The comparative is used to describe two unequal things.

> The math class is *larger than* the philosophy class.
>
> Jean is *more intelligent than* Joan.

In the first example, the *math class* is being compared with the *philosophy class,* and they are not equal. In the second example, *Jean* is being compared with *Joan,* and they are not equal.

The superlative is used when there are more than two items to compare and one of them is outstanding in some way.

> The math class is *the largest in* the school.
>
> Jean is *the most intelligent in* the class.

In the first example, the *math class* is compared with all of the other classes *in the school,* and the math class is larger than each of the other classes. In the second example, *Jean* is compared with all of the other students *in the class,* and Jean is more intelligent than each of the other students.

The following chart outlines the uses of comparatives and superlatives.

USES OF COMPARATIVES AND SUPERLATIVES	
COMPARATIVES	Are used to show the relationship between two things, and these two things are not equal.
SUPERLATIVES	Are used to show how one item is outstanding in a group of three or more.

APPENDIX EXERCISE C6: Each of the following sentences contains a comparative or superlative. Put parentheses around the comparative or superlative. Then indicate if the sentences are correct (C) or incorrect (I).

__C__ 1. We have (the friendliest) pets of all.

__I__ 2. This set of problems is (the most difficult of) the last set was.
         (*more difficult than*)

_____ 3. The grey cat has a nicest disposition than the black cat.

_____ 4. You missed the best party of the year last night.

_____ 5. Her car is the most fuel-efficient of most other cars.

_____ 6. The weather this year is the drier that it has been in a decade.

_____ 7. My boss is not the most understanding of bosses.

_____ 8. This is earlier that I have ever arrived at work.

_____ 9. The scores on the second exam were the highest of those on the first exam.

_____ 10. Cathy is more reticent than the other students in the class to volunteer answers.

APPENDIX REVIEW EXERCISE (C1–C6): Indicate if the following sentences are correct (C) or incorrect (I).

_____ 1. The new movie is not only deeply moving but also very well paced.

_____ 2. Some of the rooms were scheduled to be painted this week.

_____ 3. Please drop these letters off at the most near post office.

_____ 4. The man wrote and signed the check, presented it to the cashier, and leaving with cash.

_____ 5. The noises coming from outside the house was frightening the family inside.

_____ 6. Today she has scheduled the more important interview of her career.

_____ 7. Your excuses are neither credible nor acceptable.

_____ 8. Half of your answers on the exam were less than adequate.

_____ 9. Hal is trying to behave in a more honorabler way than he has in the past.

_____ 10. After dinner, we can take a walk, play a game, or go bowling.

_____ 11. The stairs leading to the top floor of the building is blocked now.

_____ 12. This is a more ridiculous plan than you have ever made.

_____ 13. The politician claimed that he had neither asked for nor accepted any illegal donations.

_____ 14. I believe that most of the reasons presented in the report was convincing.

_____ 15. The trip by train is longer but less expensive than the trip by plane.

VERB FORMS

You should be familiar with the following verb forms: the base form, the third-person singular form, the past form, the past participle, and the present participle.

BASE FORM	THIRD-PERSON SINGULAR	PAST FORM	PAST PARTICIPLE	PRESENT PARTICIPLE
walk	walks	walked	walked	walking
hear	hears	heard	heard	hearing
take	takes	took	taken	taking
begin	begins	began	begun	beginning
come	comes	came	come	coming
think	thinks	thought	thought	thinking

You should be particularly aware of the following three problematic situations with verb forms because they are the most common and the easiest to correct: (1) using the correct form after *have*, (2) using the correct form after *be*, and (3) using the correct form after modals.

Appendix C7: AFTER *HAVE,* USE THE PAST PARTICIPLE

The verb *have* in any of its forms (*have, has, had, having*) can be followed by another verb. Whenever you use the verb *have* in any of its forms, you should be sure that a verb that follows it is in the past participle form.

They *had walk** to school.	(should be *had walked*)
We *have see** the show.	(should be *have seen*)
He *has took** the test.	(should be *has taken*)
*Having ate**, he went to school.	(should be *Having eaten*)
She *should have did** the work.	(should be *should have done*)

In addition, you should be sure that, if you have a subject and a past participle, you also have a form of the verb *have.*

My friend *sung** in the choir.	(should be *sang* or *has sung*)
He *become** angry at his friend.	(should be *became* or *has become*)
The boat *sunk** in the ocean.	(should be *sank* or *has sunk*)

The following chart outlines the use of verb forms after *have.*

VERB FORMS AFTER *HAVE*
have + past participle

APPENDIX EXERCISE C7: Each of the following sentences contains a verb formed with *have.* Underline the verbs twice, and study the forms following *have.* Then indicate if the sentences are correct (C) or incorrect (I).

__I__   1. Her sisters <u>have came</u> to help plan the party.
         (have come)

__C__   2. I <u>thought</u> that I <u>had told</u> you everything.

_____   3. The girl has wore the same dress to school each day this week.

_____   4. High winds have blown the plane off course.

_____   5. The computer cartridge has running out of ink.

_____   6. Lightning had struck and had knocked the tree down.

_____   7. Perhaps you have drew the wrong conclusion.

_____   8. The professor has taught this course many times before.

_____   9. The surprised student had not knew that there was an exam that day.

_____ 10. All the family members have always gotten together to celebrate Thanksgiving.

Appendix C8: AFTER *BE,* USE THE PRESENT PARTICIPLE OR THE PAST PARTICIPLE

The verb *be* in any of its forms (*am, is, are, was, were, be, been, being*) can be followed by another verb. This verb should be in the present participle or past participle form.

We *are do** our homework.	(should be *are doing*)
The homework *was do** early.	(should be *was done*)
Tom *is take** the book.	(should be *is taking*)

The following chart outlines the use of verb forms after *be*.

VERB FORMS AFTER *BE*
be   +   (1) present participle (2) past participle

APPENDIX EXERCISE C8: Each of the following sentences contains a verb formed with *be*. Underline the verbs twice, and study the forms following *be*. Then indicate if the sentences are correct (C) or incorrect (I).

__I__   1. The new president <u>will be inaugurate</u> next week.
(will be inaugurated)

__C__   2. The plans that <u>were presented</u> last week <u>are unchanged</u>.

_____   3. The photograph was took without her permission.

_____   4. She has been promoted because of her excellent work.

_____   5. We are always arguing about what is happens in politics.

_____   6. He should not have been smoke in the office, but he was.

_____   7. The telephone was ringing constantly throughout the day.

_____   8. All of the plants were froze because of the cold weather.

_____   9. Everyone is wondering when the train will be departing.

_____ 10. The planes were take off and land right on schedule.

Appendix C9: AFTER *WILL, WOULD,* OR OTHER MODALS, USE THE BASE FORM OF THE VERB

Modals such as *will, would, shall, should, can, could, may, might,* and *must* are helping verbs that will be followed by a base form of the verb. Whenever you see a modal, you should be sure that the verb that follows it is its base form.

The boat *will leaving** at 3:00 P.M.	(should be *will leave*)
The doctor *may arrives** soon.	(should be *may arrive*)
The students *must taken** the exam.	(should be *must take*)

The following chart outlines the use of verb forms after modals.

VERB FORMS AFTER MODALS
modal + base form of the verb

APPENDIX EXERCISE C9: Each of the following sentences contains a verb formed with a modal. Underline the verbs twice, and study the forms following the modals. Then indicate if the sentences are correct (C) or incorrect (I).

_C_ 1. The professor cannot return the papers until tomorrow.

_I_ 2. The tour guide may preferring to leave within an hour.
       (may prefer)

_____ 3. The next step in the process will depends on the results of the medical tests.

_____ 4. He asked if you might be coming to the party.

_____ 5. The team members must to try a lot harder in the second half of the game.

_____ 6. My friend told me that he could taken care of the problem.

_____ 7. When do you think the company might announce its decision?

_____ 8. The teaching assistant must not gave the students any more time for the test.

_____ 9. Many of the cars on the lot will going on sale this weekend.

_____ 10. He was angry because his car would not start this morning.

VERB USES

Many different problems in using verb tenses are possible in English. Three of them occur frequently, so you need to pay careful attention to them: (1) knowing when to use the past with the present, (2) using *had* and *have* tenses correctly, and (3) using the correct tense with time expressions.

Appendix C10: KNOW WHEN TO USE THE PAST WITH THE PRESENT

One common verb tense problem is the switch from the past tense to the present tense for no particular reason. Often, when a sentence has both a past tense and a present tense, the sentence is incorrect.

> He *took* the money when he *wants** it.

This sentence says that *he took the money* (in the past) *when he wants it* (in the present). This sentence does not make sense because it is impossible to do something in the past as a result of wanting it in the present. This sentence can be corrected in several ways, depending on the desired meaning.

> He *took* the money when he *wanted* it.
>
> He *takes* the money when he *wants* it.

The first example means that *he took the money* (in the past) *when he wanted it* (in the past). This meaning is logical, and the sentence is correct. The second example means that *he takes the money* (habitually) *when he wants it* (habitually). This meaning is also logical, and the second example is also correct.

It is necessary to point out, however, that it is possible for a logical sentence in English to have both a present tense and a past tense.

I know that he took the money yesterday.

The meaning of this sentence is logical: *I know* (right now, in the present) that he *took the money* (yesterday, in the past). You can see from this example that it is possible for an English sentence to have both a present tense and a past tense. When you see a sentence with both a present tense and a past tense, you must think about whether the meaning is logical or not.

The following chart outlines the use of the past tense and the present tense.

USING THE PAST WITH THE PRESENT

1. If you see a sentence with one verb in the past and one verb in the present, the sentence is probably incorrect.
2. However, it is possible for a logical sentence to have both the past and the present together.
3. If you see the past and the present together, you must check the meaning to determine whether or not the sentence is logical.

APPENDIX EXERCISE C10: Each of the following sentences has at least one verb in the past and one verb in the present. Underline the verbs twice, and decide if the meanings are logical. Then indicate if the sentences are correct (C) or incorrect (I).

__I__ 1. The audience members <u>need</u> to take their seats because the play <u>was</u> about to start. *(is)*

__C__ 2. Today's newspaper <u>has</u> a story that <u>describes</u> what <u>happened</u> during the tragedy.

_____ 3. When he told her the truth, she is pleased with what she heard.

_____ 4. The teacher is well aware that the students did not understand the assignment.

_____ 5. I had problems in my last math course, but this one is going much better.

_____ 6. Every morning Rob leaves the house at the same time and took the bus to work.

_____ 7. As the plane was landing, the passengers remain in their seats with their seat belts fastened.

_____ 8. The police are certain that the suspect committed the crime.

_____ 9. On the way home from work, they filled the car up with gas and then heads to the supermarket.

_____ 10. People understand what happened, but they are unclear about why it occurred this way.

Appendix C11: USE *HAVE* AND *HAD* CORRECTLY

Two tenses that are often confused are the present perfect (*have* + past participle) and the past perfect (*had* + past participle). These two tenses have completely different uses, and you should understand how to differentiate them.

The present perfect (*have* + past participle) can refer to the period of time *from the past until the present.*

> Sue *has lived* in Los Angeles for ten years.

This sentence means that Sue has lived in Los Angeles for the ten years up to the present. According to this sentence, Sue is still living in Los Angeles.

Because the present perfect can refer to a period of time from the past until the present, it is not correct in a sentence that indicates past only.

> *At the start of the nineteenth century,* Thomas Jefferson *has become**
> president of the United States.

In this example, the phrase *at the start of the nineteenth century* indicates that the action of the verb was in the past only, but the verb indicates the period of time from the past until the present. Since this is not logical, the sentence is not correct. The verb *has become* should be changed to *became.*

The past perfect (*had* + past participle) refers to a period of time that *started in the past and ended in the past, before something else happened in the past.*

> Sue *had lived* in Los Angeles for ten years when she *moved* to San Diego.

This sentence means that Sue lived in Los Angeles for ten years in the past, before she moved to San Diego. She no longer lives in Los Angeles.

Because the past perfect begins in the past and ends in the past, it is generally not correct in the same sentence with the present tense.

> Tom *had finished* the exam when the teacher *collects** the papers.

This sentence indicates that *Tom finished the exam* (in the past), and that action ended in the past at the same time that *the teacher collects the papers* (in the present). This sentence is not logical, so the sentence is not correct.

The following chart outlines the uses of the present perfect and the past perfect.

USING (*HAVE* + PAST PARTICIPLE) AND (*HAD* + PAST PARTICIPLE)			
TENSE	FORM	MEANING	USE
present perfect	*have* + past participle	past up to now	not with a past tense**
past perfect	*had* + past participle	before past	not with a present tense
**Except when the time expression *since* is part of the sentence (see C12).			

APPENDIX EXERCISE C11: Each of the following sentences contains *had* or *have*. Underline the verbs twice and decide if the meanings are logical. Then indicate if the sentences are correct (C) or incorrect (I).

__C__ 1. She <u>is</u> very pleased that her son <u>has graduated</u> with honors.

__I__ 2. After the bell <u>had rung</u>, the students <u>leave</u> class quickly.
(left)

_____ 3. I have visited that museum each time that I traveled to the city.

_____ 4. The lawyer suddenly found out that he had made a big mistake.

_____ 5. Admissions are based on what you have done throughout your high school years.

_____ 6. When all the papers had been collected, the teacher dismisses the class.

_____ 7. The garden was not growing well because there had not been much rain for months.

_____ 8. She knows that you have always tried to be helpful.

_____ 9. I can tell you what I know about what has transpired during the investigation.

_____ 10. We will be able to discuss the situation thoroughly after you have submitted your report.

Appendix C12: USE THE CORRECT TENSE WITH TIME EXPRESSIONS

When a time expression is used in a sentence, it commonly indicates what tense is needed in the sentence.

> We <u>moved</u> to New York *in 1998*.
>
> We <u>had left</u> there *by 2002*.
>
> We <u>have lived</u> in San Francisco *since 2004*.

In the first example, the time expression *in 1998* indicates that the verb should be in the simple past (*moved*). In the second example, the time expression *by 2002* indicates that the verb should be in the past perfect (*had left*). In the third example, the time expression *since 2004* indicates that the verb should be in the present perfect (*have lived*).

Some additional time expressions that clearly indicate the correct tense are *ago, last,* and *lately*.

> She <u>got</u> a job *two years ago*.
>
> She <u>started</u> working *last week*.
>
> She <u>has worked</u> very hard *lately*.

In the first example, the time expression *two years ago* indicates that the verb should be in the simple past (*got*). In the second example, the time expression *last week* indicates that the verb should be in the simple past (*started*). In the third example, the time expression *lately* indicates that the verb should be in the present perfect (*has worked*).

The following chart lists time expressions that indicate the correct verb tense.

USING CORRECT TENSES WITH TIME EXPRESSIONS		
PAST PERFECT	SIMPLE PAST	PRESENT PERFECT
by (1920)	*(one century) ago* *in (1920)* *last (century)*	*since (1920)* *lately*

APPENDIX EXERCISE C12: Each of the following sentences contains a time expression. Put parentheses around the time expressions, and underline the verbs twice. Then indicate if the sentences are correct (C) or incorrect (I).

___I___ 1. (By 1995), Steve <u>has decided</u> to pursue a different career.
(had decided)

___C___ 2. This university <u>was established</u> (in 1900), at the turn of the last century.

_____ 3. Since I last saw you, I got a job at the United Nations.

_____ 4. Mike has applied to law school a few months ago.

_____ 5. The organization elected new officers just last month.

_____ 6. We experienced problem after problem lately.

_____ 7. By the end of the meeting, all of the participants had reached an agreement.

_____ 8. Sara has finally graduated from the university in June.

_____ 9. I am living in the same neighborhood since I was a child.

_____ 10. I was glad that you called me because I tried to call you just a few minutes ago and got a busy signal.

PASSIVE VERBS

In a passive sentence, the subject and object are reversed from where they are found in an active sentence. A passive verb consists of a form of the verb *be* and a past participle, and *by* is used in front of the object in a passive verb.

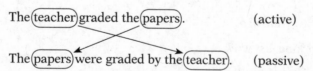

The (teacher) graded the (papers).   (active)

The (papers) were graded by the (teacher).   (passive)

The first example is an active statement, and the second example is a passive statement. The subject from the active statement (*teacher*) has become the object following *by* in the passive example; the object from the active example (*papers*) has become the subject in the passive example. The verb in the passive example consists of a form of *be* (*were*) and a past participle (*graded*).

It should be noted that, in a passive sentence, *by + object* does not need to be included to have a complete sentence.

> The papers were graded by the teacher.
>
> The papers were graded.

Each of these examples is a correct sentence. The first example is a passive statement that includes *by the teacher*. The second example is a passive statement that does not include *by*.

You should pay attention to the passive in your English. You should pay attention to (1) the form of the passive, and (2) the use of the passive.

Appendix C13: USE THE CORRECT FORM OF THE PASSIVE

One possible problem with the passive is an incorrect form of the passive. A correctly formed passive will always have a form of *be* and a past participle. The following are examples of common errors in the form of the passive.

> The portrait *was painting** by a famous artist.
>
> The project *will finished** by the group.

In the first example, the passive is formed incorrectly because the past participle *painted* should be used rather than the present participle *painting*. In the second example, the verb *be* has not been included, and some form of *be* is necessary for a passive verb. The verb in the second example should be *will be finished*.

The following chart outlines the way to form the passive correctly.

THE FORM OF THE PASSIVE
be + past participle

APPENDIX EXERCISE C13: Each of the following sentences has a passive meaning. Underline twice the verbs that should be passive. Then indicate if the sentences are correct (C) or incorrect (I).

__I__ 1. The trees and hedges <u>will be trim</u> this week.
      (will be trimmed)

__C__ 2. That kind of decision <u>is made</u> by the board of directors.

_____ 3. The bank robbed yesterday by a masked gunman.

_____ 4. The plans for the building complex were describing by the architect.

_____ 5. The oil has been changed, and the tires have been filled with air.

_____ 6. Some tickets to the concert have given away by the concert promoters.

_____ 7. As soon as the food was cooked, it was brought to the table.

_____ 8. The money for the purchase was accepted the clerk.

_____ 9. Students will not be allowed to register if their fees have not been pay.

_____ 10. The election is being held, and the results will be posted by the election committee.

Appendix C14: RECOGNIZE ACTIVE AND PASSIVE MEANINGS

When there is no object (with or without *by*) after a verb, you must look at the meaning of the sentence to determine if the verb should be active or passive. Look at the following examples.

> We <u>mailed</u> the *package* at the post office.
>
> The letter <u>was mailed</u> *by us* today before noon.
>
> The letter <u>was mailed</u> today before noon.
>
> The letter <u>mailed</u>* today before noon.

The first three examples are all correct. The first example has the active verb *mailed* used with the object *package*; the second example has the passive verb *was mailed* used with *by us*; the third example has the passive verb *was mailed* used without an object. The last example is not correct. The verb *mailed* looks like a correct active verb, but a passive verb is needed. There is no *by* and an object to tell you that a passive verb is needed; instead, you must understand from the meaning that it is incorrect. You should ask yourself *if the letter mails itself* (the letter *does* the action) or if *someone mails the letter* (the letter *receives* the action of being mailed). Since a letter does not mail itself, the passive is required in this sentence. The verb in the last example should be changed from the active *mailed* to the passive *was mailed*.

The following chart outlines the difference in meaning between active and passive verbs.

ACTIVE AND PASSIVE MEANINGS	
ACTIVE	The subject does the action of the verb.
PASSIVE	The subject receives the action of the verb.

APPENDIX EXERCISE C14: Each of the following sentences contains at least one active verb; however, some of the verbs should be passive. Underline the verbs twice. Then indicate if the sentences are correct (C) or incorrect (I).

_I_ 1. The game <u>won</u> in overtime.
   (was won)

_C_ 2. The engine <u>started</u> on the very first try.

_____ 3. The photos placed in frames on the mantle.

_____ 4. The top students selected to receive scholarships.

_____ 5. The store opened right on schedule.

_____ 6. The outcome expected because of the lack of effort.

_____ 7. The comedian's jokes amused the audience.

_____ 8. The policy changes announced late yesterday afternoon.

_____ 9. The chair knocked over, and the child fell off.

_____ 10. The surgical procedure lasted for more than six hours.

APPENDIX REVIEW EXERCISE (C7–C14): Indicate if the following sentences are correct (C) or incorrect (I).

_____ 1. The director may has to cut a few of the more violent scenes from the movie.

_____ 2. He feels the way that he does today because of what happened in the past.

_____ 3. The vegetables washed and chopped up for salad.

_____ 4. The children have drank all of the milk from the refrigerator.

_____ 5. The family did not take any long vacations lately.

_____ 6. It is expects that many of the employees will be transferred to new positions.

_____ 7. The company was found more than a hundred years ago.

_____ 8. The report clearly proved that no one had been treated unfairly.

_____ 9. I would like to know when you will be able to give me the money.

_____ 10. The home owner knew that he has paid his insurance premiums on time.

_____ 11. I am worrying about the decisions that I am try to make.

_____ 12. By the end of the final talk, the lecturer has managed to convey his main points.

_____ 13. I am satisfied that you did everything possible to resolve the problem.

_____ 14. I had sought advice from my counselor before I registered for classes.

_____ 15. The story appeared in the newspaper soon after the politician interviewed.

NOUNS

A noun is the part of speech that is used to refer to a person, place, thing (or idea). Two issues related to nouns are (1) whether they are singular or plural, and (2) whether they are countable or uncountable.

Appendix C15: USE THE CORRECT SINGULAR OR PLURAL NOUN

A common problem with nouns is whether to use a singular or a plural noun.

> On the table there were many _dish*_.
>
> The lab assistant finished every _tests*_.

In the first example, _many_ indicates that the plural _dishes_ is needed. In the second example, _every_ indicates that the singular _test_ is needed.

You should watch very carefully for key words such as *each, every, one, single,* and *a* that indicate that a noun should be singular. You should also watch carefully for such key words as *many, several, both, various,* and *two* (or any other number except *one*) that indicate that a noun should be plural.

The following chart lists the key words that indicate to you whether a noun should be singular or plural.

KEY WORDS FOR SINGULAR AND PLURAL NOUNS					
FOR SINGULAR NOUNS	*each*	*every*	*single*	*one*	*a*
FOR PLURAL NOUNS	*both*	*two*	*many*	*several*	*various*

APPENDIX EXERCISE C15: Each of the following sentences contains at least one key word to tell you if a noun should be singular or plural. Put parentheses around the key words. Underline the nouns they describe. Then indicate if the sentences are correct (C) or incorrect (I).

__I__ 1. (Each) <u>exhibits</u> in the zoo is open today.
 (exhibit)

__C__ 2. (Both) <u>children</u> have (various) <u>assignments</u> to complete tonight.

_____ 3. Would you like a single scoop of ice cream or two scoops?

_____ 4. She must take several pills every days.

_____ 5. Final exam week is an exhausting time for many students.

_____ 6. Various plans for a new community centers have been offered.

_____ 7. Every times that I go there, I run into several acquaintances.

_____ 8. A single serving at this restaurant consists of more food than one people can consume.

_____ 9. One incident last week caused many misunderstandings.

_____ 10. There are several candidates for the position, and each ones of them is extremely qualified.

Appendix C16: DISTINGUISH COUNTABLE AND UNCOUNTABLE NOUNS

In English, nouns are classified as either countable or uncountable. It is necessary to distinguish countable and uncountable nouns in order to use the correct modifiers with them.

As the name implies, countable nouns are nouns that can be counted. Countable nouns can come in quantities of one, or two, or a hundred, and so forth. The noun *book* is countable because you can have one book or several books.

Uncountable nouns, on the other hand, are nouns that cannot be counted because they come in some indeterminate quantity or mass. A noun such as *happiness* cannot be counted; you cannot have one happiness or two happinesses.

It is important for you to recognize the difference between countable and uncountable nouns when you come across such key words as *much* and *many*.

> He has seen *much** foreign *films*.
>
> He did not have *many** *fun* at the movies.

In the first example, *much* is incorrect because *films* is countable. This example should say *many foreign films*. In the second example, *many* is incorrect because *fun* is uncountable. This example should say *much fun*.

The following chart lists the key word that indicate to you whether a noun should be countable or uncountable.

KEY WORDS FOR COUNTABLE AND UNCOUNTABLE NOUNS				
FOR COUNTABLE NOUNS	*many*	*number*	*few*	*fewer*
FOR UNCOUNTABLE NOUNS	*much*	*amount*	*little*	*less*

APPENDIX EXERCISE C16: Each of the following sentences contains at least one key word to tell you if a noun should be countable or uncountable. Put parentheses around the key words. Underline the nouns they describe. Then indicate if the sentences are correct (C) or incorrect (I).

__C__ 1. (Many) <u>applicants</u> came to see about the job.

__I__ 2. Today, there is an unusually large (amount) of <u>people</u> in the room.
(number)

_____ 3. Few suggestions and little help were offered.

_____ 4. We need to have more opportunities and less restrictions.

_____ 5. The official gave us much sincere assurances that we would receive assistance.

_____ 6. A large number of the facts in the report are being disputed.

_____ 7. I have less concern than she does about the much unpaid bills.

_____ 8. There are fewer men than women serving on the committee.

_____ 9. Of the many potential problems, only a little have been resolved.

_____ 10. A huge amount of paper was used to prepare the report.

PRONOUNS

Pronouns are words such as *he, us,* or *them* that take the place of nouns. The following pronoun problems are quite common: (1) distinguishing subject and object pronouns, (2) distinguishing possessive pronouns and possessive determiners, and (3) checking pronoun reference for agreement.

Appendix C17: DISTINGUISH SUBJECT AND OBJECT PRONOUNS

Subject and object pronouns can easily be confused, so you need to think carefully about these pronouns.

PRONOUNS	
SUBJECT	OBJECT
I	me
you	you
he	him
she	her
it	it
we	us
they	them

A subject pronoun is used as the subject of a verb. An object pronoun can be used as the object of a preposition. Compare the following two examples.

> Sally gave the book to John.
>
> *She* gave it to *him*.

In the second sentence, the subject pronoun *she* is replacing the noun *Sally*. The object of the verb *it* is replacing the noun *book,* and the object of the preposition *him* is replacing the noun *John.*

The following are examples of the types of subject or object pronoun errors you might see.

> *Him and me** are going to the movies.
>
> The secret is between *you and I**.

In the first example, the object pronouns *him and me* are incorrect because these pronouns serve as the subject of the verb *are.* The object pronouns *him and me* should be changed to *he and I.* In the second example, the subject pronouns *you and I* are incorrect because these pronouns serve as the object of the preposition *between.* The subject pronouns *you and I* should be changed to *you and me.*

APPENDIX EXERCISE C17: Each of the following sentences contains at least one subject or object pronoun. Put parentheses around the pronouns. Then indicate if the sentences are correct (C) or incorrect (I).

__I__ 1. (Him) and (me) are going to be taking the early bus today.
   (He and I)

__C__ 2. (We) will talk to (them), and (they) will listen to (us).

_____ 3. Just between you and I, I think that they made the best decision.

_____ 4. He and she have agreed to assist us with the project that we are trying to complete.

_____ 5. You and I have to try harder to do more for he and her.

_____ 6. It is difficult for we students to complete so many projects.

_____ 7. She said that I did not give it to her, but I am sure that she is wrong.

_____ 8. They sent you and I an invitation, so I think that we should attend the party.

_____ 9. It is not about us; instead, it is all about him and her.

_____ 10. They could not have done any more to help you and I.

Appendix C18: DISTINGUISH POSSESSIVE DETERMINERS AND PRONOUNS

Possessive determiners (or adjectives) and pronouns both show who or what "owns" a noun. However, possessive determiners and possessive pronouns do not have the same function, and these two kinds of possessives can easily be confused. A possessive determiner (or adjective) describes a noun: it must be accompanied by a noun. A possessive pronoun takes the place of a noun. It cannot be accompanied by a noun.

> They lent me *their book*.
>
> They lent me *theirs*.

In the first example, the possessive determiner *their* is accompanied by the noun *book*. In the second example, the possessive pronoun *theirs* is not accompanied by a noun.

The following are examples of errors that are possible with possessive determiners and pronouns.

> Each morning they read *theirs** newspapers.
>
> Could you lend me *your**?

In the first example, the possessive pronoun *theirs* is incorrect because it is accompanied by the noun *newspapers*, and a possessive pronoun cannot be accompanied by a noun. The possessive determiner *their* is needed in the first example. In the second example, the possessive determiner *your* is incorrect because it is not accompanied by a noun, and a possessive determiner must be accompanied by a noun. The possessive pronoun *yours* is needed.

The following chart outlines the possessives and their uses.

POSSESSIVES	
DETERMINERS	PRONOUNS
my	mine
your	yours
his	his
her	hers
its	—
our	ours
their	theirs
must be accompanied by a noun	may not be accompanied by a noun

APPENDIX EXERCISE C18: Each of the following sentences contains at least one possessive pronoun or adjective. Put parentheses around the possessives. Then indicate if the sentences are correct (C) or incorrect (I).

__I__   1. We must do (our) part to encourage (ours) teammates.
      (our teammates)

__C__   2. I will pick up (your) children when I go to pick up (mine).

_____   3. I am worried about both his response and hers.

_____   4. She lost her notes, so she asked to borrow my.

_____   5. Your explanation is, in my opinion, a bit weak.

_____   6. Why don't you show them where theirs offices are?

_____   7. It was my mistake and not your.

_____   8. He thinks that his argument is more convincing than hers.

_____   9. If these are not ours keys, then they must be theirs.

_____ 10. Do you think that your answer is better than hers or that her answer is better than yours?

Appendix C19: CHECK PRONOUN REFERENCE FOR AGREEMENT

After you have checked that the subject and object pronouns and the possessives are used correctly, you should also check each of these pronouns and possessives for agreement. The following are examples of errors of this type.

> The *boys* will cause trouble if you let *him**.
>
> *Everyone* must give *their** name.

In the first example, the singular pronoun *him* is incorrect because it refers back to the plural noun *boys*. This pronoun should be replaced with the plural pronoun *them*. In the second example, the plural possessive adjective *their* is incorrect because it refers back to the singular *everyone*. This adjective should be replaced with the singular *his or her*.

The following chart outlines what you should remember about checking pronoun reference.

PRONOUN AGREEMENT
1. Be sure that every pronoun and possessive agrees with the noun it refers to.
2. You generally check back in the sentence for agreement.

APPENDIX EXERCISE C19: Each of the following sentences contains at least one pronoun or possessive. Put parentheses around the pronouns and possessives. Underline any nouns they refer to. Then indicate if the sentences are correct (C) or incorrect (I).

<u>I</u>   1. <u>Papers</u> are due today at 5:00 P.M.; be sure to turn (it) in on time.
       (them)

<u>C</u>   2. The <u>party</u> is for (my) <u>neighbors</u>, and (they) know all about (it).

_____   3. Everyone must submit an application if you want to be considered for the

       scholarship.

_____   4. The concert is tonight, and we will be going with our friends to hear them.

_____   5. The sunshine today is lovely; I enjoy feeling it on my face.

_____   6. The man has a problem, and he will have to resolve it all by herself.

_____   7. My friend has a book on that subject, and she said that I could borrow her.

_____   8. Your brothers have the money, and they know that you want it for yourself.

_____   9. Each person has their own individual set of fingerprints.

_____   10. Your classmates will have to finish the project by yourselves.

APPENDIX REVIEW EXERCISE (C15–C19): Indicate if the following sentences are correct (C) or incorrect (I).

_____   1. She has tried much times to raise a little extra money.

_____   2. We saw them getting into their car.

_____   3. Of the two assignments, only one is complete; the other one has many errors in it.

_____   4. Him and her never even asked us to lend them the money.

_____   5. She told him about her decision, and he expressed his dissatisfaction with it.

_____   6. Few issues have raised so many problems.

_____   7. I have numerous questions about the situation, and I hope you can answer it.

_____   8. You and I should not open this package because it was not given to you and I.

_____   9. Many students have tried for perfect grades, but little of them have succeeded.

_____   10. Our friends are coming to visit us after they visit their parents.

_____   11. It will take a miracle to meet the various need of each person in the room.

_____   12. They saw you and me, but we did not see them even though they called out to us.

_____   13. You have done your part, but they have not done their.

_____   14. This diet food has less fat and less calories.

_____   15. We have our reasons, and they have theirs.

ADJECTIVES AND ADVERBS

An adjective is a modifier that is used to describe a noun or pronoun, while an adverb is a modifier that is used to describe a verb, an adjective, or another adverb.

> He is a *nice* man, and he is *generous*.
>
> He is *really* generous, and he *almost always* has a smile on his face.

In the first example, the adjective *nice* is describing the noun *man*, and the adjective *generous* is describing the pronoun *he*. In the second example, the adverb *really* is describing the adjective *generous*, the adverb *almost* is describing the adverb *always*, and the adverb *always* is describing the verb *has*.

Three issues with adjectives and adverbs that it is important to master are the following: (1) the basic uses of adjectives and adverbs, (2) the correct positioning of adjectives and adverbs, and (3) the use of *-ed* and *-ing* verbal adjectives.

Appendix C20: USE BASIC ADJECTIVES AND ADVERBS CORRECTLY

Adjectives and adverbs have very different uses. Adjectives describe nouns and pronouns, and adverbs describe verbs, adjectives, and other adverbs. The following are examples of incorrectly used adjectives and adverbs.

> They were seated at a *largely** table.
>
> The child talked *quick** to her mother.
>
> We read an *extreme** long story.

In the first example, the adverb *largely* is incorrect because the adjective *large* is needed to describe the noun *table*. In the second example, the adjective *quick* is incorrect because the adverb *quickly* is needed to describe the verb *talked*. In the last example, the adjective *extreme* is incorrect because the adverb *extremely* is needed to describe the adjective *long*.

The following chart outlines the important information that you should remember about the basic uses of adjectives and adverbs.

BASIC USES OF ADJECTIVES AND ADVERBS	
ADJECTIVES	Describe nouns or pronouns.
ADVERBS	Describe verbs, adjectives, or other adverbs.

APPENDIX EXERCISE C20: Each of the following sentences has at least one adjective or adverb. Put parentheses around the adjectives and adverbs, and indicate which words they describe. Then indicate if the sentences are correct (C) or incorrect (I).

_____ 1. The race was held under (extreme) (humid) conditions.

    extreme describes humid

    humid describes conditions

    (extremely)

_____ 2. The hungry baby wailed quite plaintively.

    hungry describes baby

    quite describes plaintively

    plaintively describes wailed

_____ 3. We saw a real exciting movie with an unexpected ending.

    _____

    _____

    _____

_____ 4. The striking workers marched slowly and deliberately outside of the locked front gates of the company.

    _____

    _____

    _____

_____ 5. The manager studied the complex issue thoroughly before making the difficultly decision.

    _____

    _____

    _____

_____ 6. The parking lot had recently been resurfaced with thick black asphalt.

    _____

    _____

    _____

_____ 7. We proceeded extremely cautious in order to arrive at a totally acceptable outcome.

    _____

    _____

    _____

_____ 8. The couple decided rather suddenly to alter the plans for their vacation considerable.

    _____

    _____

    _____

_____ 9. The large white building at the end of the circular driveway houses the main office.

_____

_____

_____

_____ 10. Whose brilliantly idea was it to take this supposed shortcut when none of us actually knew where it led?

_____

_____

_____

Appendix C21: POSITION ADJECTIVES AND ADVERBS CORRECTLY

It is important to pay attention to the position of both adjectives and adverbs. In English, a one-word adjective comes before the noun. Look at this example of an incorrectly positioned adjective.

> The information _important_* is on the first page.

In this example, the adjective _important_ should come before the noun _information_ because _important_ describes _information_.

Adverbs can be used in many different positions in English, but there is at least one position where an adverb cannot be used. If a verb has an object, then an adverb describing the verb cannot be used between the verb and its object. Look at these examples.

> The man drove _quickly_.
>
> The man drove _quickly_* the car.

In the first example, the adverb _quickly_ describes the verb _drove_. It is positioned correctly after the verb _drove_ because _drove_ does not have an object. In the second example, the adverb _quickly_ is incorrectly positioned. The adverb _quickly_ describes the verb _drove_, but the adverb cannot come directly after the verb because the verb has an object (_car_). A possible correction for the last example would be _the man drove the car quickly_.

The following chart outlines the key information you should remember about the position of adjectives and adverbs.

THE POSITION OF ADJECTIVES AND ADVERBS	
ADJECTIVES	A one-word adjective comes before the noun it describes.
ADVERBS	An adverb can appear in many positions. One place that an adverb cannot be used is between the verb it describes and the object of the verb.

APPENDIX EXERCISE C21: Each of the following sentences has at least one adjective or adverb. Put parentheses around the adjectives and adverbs, and indicate which words they describe. Then indicate if the sentences are correct (C) or incorrect (I).

__I__   1. Can you return (immediately) the necklace?

     immediately describes return

     (return the necklace immediately)

__C__   2. He is a (serious) man who (always) works (diligently).

     serious describes man

     always describes works

     diligently describes works

_____   3. The worried mother gently scolded the little girl.

_____   4. He uses often his checks to pay for purchases.

_____   5. The lifeguard attentive jumped quickly into the pool.

_____   6. In the paper, you need to explain the reasons for your hypothesis more clearly.

_____   7. The accountant studied carefully the figures before preparing the monthly report.

_____   8. The lawyer skillfully questioned the hostile witness.

_____ 9. I cannot remember always the number of the account.

_____

_____

_____

_____ 10. The temperature dropped suddenly, and the people local bundled up to face the

chilly weather.

_____

_____

_____

Appendix C22: USE -*ED* AND -*ING* ADJECTIVES CORRECTLY

Verb forms ending in -*ed* and -*ing* can be used as adjectives. For example, the verbal adjectives *cleaned* and *cleaning* come from the verb *to clean*.

> The woman *cleans* the car.
>
> The *cleaning* woman worked on the car.
>
> The woman put the *cleaned* car back in the garage.

In the first example, *cleans* is the verb of the sentence. In the second example, *cleaning* is a verbal adjective describing *woman*. In the third example *cleaned* is a verbal adjective describing *car*.

Look at the following examples of incorrectly used -*ing* and -*ed* adjectives.

> The *cleaning** car...
>
> The *cleaned** woman...

The difference between an -*ed* adjective and an -*ing* adjective is similar to the difference between the active and the passive (see C13–C14). An -*ing* adjective (like the active) means that the noun it describes is doing the action. The example above about the *cleaning car* is not correct because a car cannot do the action of cleaning: you cannot say that a car cleans itself. An -*ed* adjective (like the passive) means that the noun it describes is receiving the action from the verb. The example above about the *cleaned woman* is not correct because in this example a woman cannot receive the action of the verb *clean*; this sentence does not mean that *someone cleaned the woman*. To correct the examples above, you should say *the cleaned car* and *the cleaning woman*.

The following chart outlines the key information that you should remember about -*ed* and -*ing* adjectives.

-*ED* AND -*ING* ADJECTIVES			
TYPE	MEANING	USE	EXAMPLE
-*ing*	active	It does the action of the verb.	the happily *playing* children
-*ed*	passive	It receives the action of the verb.	the frequently *played* CD

APPENDIX EXERCISE C22: Each of the following sentences contains either an *-ed* or an *-ing* verbal adjective. Put parentheses around the verbal adjectives, and indicate which words they describe. Then indicate if the sentences are correct (C) or incorrect (I).

__C__ 1. The line is long, but at least it is a (fast-moving) line.

fast-moving describes line

__I__ 2. The (satisfying) customers thanked the salesperson for the good service.

satisfying describes customers

(satisfied)

_____ 3. The people felt shocked as they heard the disturbed news.

_____ 4. The delighted girl thanked her friend for the unexpected gift.

_____ 5. It was such a depressed situation that no one smiled.

_____ 6. The snow-capped mountains ringed the charmed village.

_____ 7. An annoying guest made a number of rude comments to the frustrated host.

_____ 8. The correcting papers are being returned to the waiting students.

_____ 9. An unidentified attacker tried to rob the strolling couple.

_____

_____

_____

_____ 10. The most requesting room in the hotel is the one with the unobstructing view of the lake.

_____

_____

_____

ARTICLES

Articles are very difficult to learn because there are many rules, many exceptions, and many special cases. It is possible, however, to learn a few rules that will help you to use articles correctly much of the time.

Nouns in English can be either countable or uncountable. If a noun is countable, it must be either singular or plural. In addition to these general types of nouns, there are two types of articles: definite (specific) and indefinite (general).

ARTICLES	COUNTABLE SINGULAR NOUNS	COUNTABLE PLURAL NOUNS	UNCOUNTABLE NOUNS
INDEFINITE (General)	*a* pen *an* apple	___ pens ___ apples	___ ink ___ juice
DEFINITE (Specific)	*the* pen *the* apple	*the* pens *the* apples	*the* ink *the* juice

Appendix C23: USE ARTICLES WITH SINGULAR NOUNS

You can see from the chart that if a noun is either countable plural or uncountable, it is possible to have either the definite article *the* or no article (indefinite). With all countable singular nouns, however, you must have an article unless you already have another determiner such as *my* or *each*.

I have *money*.	(uncountable — no article needed)
I have *books*.	(countable plural — no article needed)
I have *a book*.	(countable singular — article needed)

The following chart outlines the key information that you should remember about articles with singular nouns.

ARTICLES WITH SINGULAR NOUNS
A singular noun must have an article (*a, an, the*) or some other determiner such as *my* or *each*. (A plural noun or uncountable noun may or may not have an article.)

APPENDIX EXERCISE C23: The following sentences contain different types of nouns. Underline the countable singular nouns. Put parentheses around any articles in front of the countable singular nouns. Then indicate if the sentences are correct (C) or incorrect (I).

__I__ 1. Man wearing stylish hat is standing at door.
   (*A man . . . a . . . hat . . . the door*)

__C__ 2. I am working on (a) difficult task, and I need help with it.

_____ 3. Sam is taking classes in geography, math, and science as well as holding part-time job.

_____ 4. I need advice about problems that I have been having with my neighbors.

_____ 5. She has funny feeling about surprising event that she just witnessed.

_____ 6. We would like to buy a van that has enough space for a family of six.

_____ 7. In the science course, the students must read textbook, take exams, give presentation, and participate in discussions.

_____ 8. The family likes pets; they have turtles, parakeets, snake, cats, and large dog.

_____ 9. She has a strong opinion about a situation involving acquaintances of ours.

_____ 10. Plants need water and air to grow.

Appendix C24: DISTINGUISH *A* AND *AN*

The basic difference between *a* and *an* is that *a* is used in front of consonant, and *an* is used in front of vowels (*a, e, i, o, u*).

a **b**ook	*an* **o**range
a **m**an	*an* **i**llness
a **p**age	*an* **a**utomobile

In reality, the rule is that *a* is used in front of a word that begins with a consonant *sound* and that *an* is used in front of a word that begins with a vowel *sound*. Pronounce the following examples.

a university	*a* hand	*a* one-way street	*a* euphemism	*a* xerox machine
an unhappy man	*an* hour	*an* omen	*an* event	*an* x-ray machine

These examples show that certain beginning letters can have either a consonant or a vowel sound. A word that begins with *u* can begin with the consonant sound *y* as in *university* or with a vowel sound as in *unhappy*. A word that begins with *h* can begin with a consonant *h* sound as in *hand* or with a vowel sound as in *hour*. A word that begins with *o* can begin with a consonant *w* sound as in *one* or with a vowel sound as in *omen*. A word that begins with *e* can begin with either a consonant *y* sound as in *euphemism* or with a vowel sound as in *event*. A word that begins with *x* can begin with either a consonant *z* sound as in *xerox* or with a vowel sound as in *x-ray*.

The following chart outlines the key information about the use of *a* and *an*.

A AND *AN*	
A	*A* is used in front of a singular noun that begins with a consonant sound.
AN	*An* is used in front of a singular noun that begins with a vowel sound.
Be careful with words beginning with *u, o, e, x,* or *h.* These words may begin with either a vowel or a consonant sound.	

APPENDIX EXERCISE C24: Each of the following sentences contains at least one *a* or *an*. Put parentheses around each *a* or *an*. Underline the beginning of the word that directly follows. Pronounce the word. Then indicate if the sentences are correct (C) or incorrect (I).

__C__ 1. You have (an) <u>op</u>portunity to attend (a) <u>one</u>-time event.

__I__ 2. He made (a) <u>mis</u>take, but it was (a) <u>hon</u>est mistake.
(an honest mistake)

_____ 3. They are staying in a hotel with a jacuzzi, a sauna, and a heated pool.

_____ 4. It is a honor to be a guest at such a important celebration.

_____ 5. The family is planning a once-in-a-lifetime trip to a faraway country.

_____ 6. Is this a usual occurrence or a unusual occurrence?

_____ 7. The party decorations included a colorful banner, a hand-painted sign, and a helium balloon.

_____ 8. She had an euphoric feeling after she unexpectedly won an huge sum of money.

_____ 9. A person who is unable to write may use a "X" rather than a signature when signing a document.

_____ 10. The class read a traditional story about a unicorn that saved a helpless child.

Appendix C25: MAKE ARTICLES AGREE WITH NOUNS

The definite article (*the*) is used for both singular and plural nouns, so agreement is not a problem with the definite article. However, because the use of the indefinite article is different for singular and plural nouns, you must be careful of agreement between the indefinite article and the noun. One very common agreement error is to use the singular definite article (*a* or *an*) with a plural noun.

> He saw *a** new *movies*.
>
> They traveled to *a** nearby *mountains*.
>
> Do you have *another** books*?

In these examples, you should not have *a* or *an* because the nouns are plural. The following sentences are possible corrections of the sentences above.

He saw a new movie.	(singular)
He saw new movies.	(plural)
They traveled to a nearby mountain.	(singular)
They traveled to nearby mountains.	(plural)
Do you have another book?	(singular)
Do you have other books?	(plural)

The following chart outlines the key point for you to remember about the agreement of articles with nouns.

AGREEMENT OF ARTICLES WITH NOUNS
You should never use *a* or *an* with a plural noun.

APPENDIX EXERCISE C25: Each of the following sentences contains *a* or *an*. Put parentheses around each *a* or *an*. Underline the noun that it describes. Then indicate if the sentences are correct (C) or incorrect (I).

___I___ 1. The team needs (a) new uniforms before the start of the season.
   (a new uniform OR *new uniforms)*

___C___ 2. I need to buy pens, pencils, (a) notebook, and (a) textbook.

_____ 3. They are buying a new house with a swimming pool, with a roomy balconies, and with a wonderful views from the balconies.

_____ 4. The visiting professor shared an interesting new theories.

_____ 5. The office has a computer, a phone, a table and chairs, and office supplies.

_____ 6. The mother told her children a bedtime stories, gave them gentle kisses, and then tucked them into bed.

_____ 7. She went shopping and bought a new dress, a new shoes, a new purse, and a new earrings.

_____ 8. I have a good reason for answering questions this way.

_____ 9. The hostess served her guests tea and a vanilla biscuits.

_____ 10. The executive needs a secretary to prepare reports and take phone messages.

Appendix C26: DISTINGUISH SPECIFIC AND GENERAL IDEAS

With countable singular nouns, it is possible to use either the definite or the indefinite article, but the definite and indefinite articles will have different meanings. The definite article is used to refer to one specific noun.

> Tom will bring *the* book tomorrow.
> (There is one specific book that Tom will bring tomorrow.)
>
> He will arrive on *the* first Tuesday in July.
> (There is only one first Tuesday in July.)
>
> He sailed on *the* Pacific Ocean.
> (There is only one Pacific Ocean.)

The indefinite article is used when the noun could be one of several different nouns.

> Tom will bring *a* book tomorrow.
> (Tom will bring any one book tomorrow.)
>
> He will arrive on *a* Tuesday in July.
> (He will arrive on one of the four or five Tuesdays in July.)
>
> He sailed on *an* ocean.
> (He sailed on any one of the world's oceans.)

The following chart outlines the key information that you should understand about specific and general ideas.

SPECIFIC AND GENERAL IDEAS		
A or AN	general idea	Use when there are many, and you do not know which one it is. Use when there are many, and you do not care which one.
THE	specific idea	Use when it is the only one. Use when there are many, and you know which one it is.

APPENDIX EXERCISE C26: Each of the following sentences contains one or more articles. Put parentheses around each article. Underline the noun it describes. Then indicate if the sentences are correct (C) or incorrect (I).

__I__ 1. We took (a) balloon ride over (an) African continent.
   (the African continent)

__C__ 2. Last evening, my friends and I went to see (a) movie that had (a) very unusual

   ending.

_____ 3. Today there is a big dark cloud in a sky.

_____ 4. The spacecraft that was recently launched is heading toward a planet Mars.

_____ 5. The teacher stood in a middle of the classroom and talked to the students.

_____ 6. Can you think of an idea for a topic for an interesting research paper?

_____ 7. I would like to stay in a same hotel that we stayed in a last time that we visited here.

_____ 8. A hat that you are wearing now is really quite a cute hat.

_____ 9. We won a prize for a best essay in the school's essay contest.

_____ 10. After the man standing over there was punched in a nose, he suffered a bloody nose.

APPENDIX REVIEW EXERCISE (C20–C26): Indicate if the following sentences are correct (C) or incorrect (I).

_____ 1. She offered an apology for a unbelievably rude comment.

_____ 2. The recipe calls for sugar, eggs, butter, flour, and vanilla.

_____ 3. The forgetful man misplaces often his keys.

_____ 4. An engine of the car that I am driving is making a funny noises.

_____ 5. The customer became increasingly impatient as she stood in an unmoving line.

_____ 6. A friend of mine works as an orderly in a hospital.

_____ 7. His job provides a good salary and a substantial benefits.

_____ 8. The student triumphantly finished the final part of the project and then turned the completed paper in.

_____ 9. She is taking an undergraduate course at nearby university.

_____ 10. The really angry father explained explicitly why his son's behavior was unacceptable.

_____ 11. It is delight to be a part of such a wonderful organization.

_____ 12. The unmaking beds and the unwashing dishes need some attention.

_____ 13. A dinner guest seated at the table should have a plate, a glass, a napkin, and eating utensils.

_____ 14. The teacher collected swiftly the exams from the anxious students.

_____ 15. At the school assembly this morning, a school principal gave speech to the students.

WRITING ASSESSMENT AND SCORING

For the Writing test sections in this book, it is possible to do the following:

- *assess* the skills used in the Writing Pre-Test, Writing Post-Test, Writing Mini-Tests, and Writing Complete Tests
- *score* the Writing Pre-Test, Writing Post-Test, Writing Mini-Tests, and Writing Complete Tests using the Writing Scoring Criteria
- *record* your test results

ASSESSING WRITING SKILLS

After you complete each Writing task on a Writing Pre-Test, Writing Post-Test, Writing Mini-Test, or Writing Complete Test, put checkmarks in the appropriate boxes in the following checklists. This will help you assess how well you have used the skills presented in the textbook.

		SKILL-ASSESSMENT CHECKLIST Writing Integrated Tasks: Skills 1–8								
		WRITING DIAGNOSTIC PRE-TEST, Question 1	WRITING REVIEW EXERCISE (Skills 1–8)	WRITING POST-TEST, Question 1	WRITING MINI-TEST 1, Question 1	WRITING MINI-TEST 3, Question 1	WRITING MINI-TEST 5, Question 1	WRITING MINI-TEST 7, Question 1	WRITING COMPLETE TEST 1, Question 1	WRITING COMPLETE TEST 2, Question 1
SKILL 1	I noted the **main points** of the **reading passage**.									
SKILL 2	I noted the **main points** of the **listening passage**.									
SKILL 3	I included a topic statement and supporting ideas in my **plan**.									
SKILL 4	I began with an overall **topic statement**.									
SKILL 5	I wrote a unified **supporting paragraph** on reading.									
SKILL 6	I wrote a unified **supporting paragraph** on listening.									
SKILL 7	I checked the **sentence structure** in my response.									
SKILL 8	I checked the **grammar** in my response.									

SKILL-ASSESSMENT CHECKLIST
Writing Independent Task: Skills 9–15

	WRITING DIAGNOSTIC PRE-TEST, Question 2	WRITING REVIEW EXERCISE (Skills 9–15)	WRITING POST-TEST, Question 2	WRITING MINI-TEST 2, Question 1	WRITING MINI-TEST 4, Question 1	WRITING MINI-TEST 6, Question 1	WRITING MINI-TEST 8, Question 1	WRITING COMPLETE TEST 1, Question 2	WRITING COMPLETE TEST 2, Question 2
SKILL 9 I used careful **planning** to outline my response.									
SKILL 10 I included the topic and organization in the **introduction**.									
SKILL 11 I wrote unified **supporting paragraphs**.									
SKILL 12 I used **transitions** to connect the supporting paragraphs.									
SKILL 13 I summarized the main points in the **conclusion**.									
SKILL 14 I checked the **sentence structure** in my response.									
SKILL 15 I checked the **grammar** in my response.									

SCORING THE WRITING TESTS USING THE SCORING CRITERIA

You may use the Writing Scoring Criteria to score your writing tasks on the Pre-Test, Post-Test, Mini-Tests, and Complete Tests. You will receive a score of 0 through 5 for each Writing task; this score of 0 through 5 will then be converted to a scaled score out of 30. The criteria for Writing scores of 0 through 5 are listed below.

WRITING SCORING CRITERIA		
5	ANSWER TO QUESTION	The student answers the question thoroughly.
	COMPREHENSIBILITY	The student can be understood completely.
	ORGANIZATION	The student's response is maturely organized and developed.
	FLOW OF IDEAS	The student's ideas flow cohesively.
	GRAMMAR	The student uses advanced grammatical structures with a high degree of accuracy.
	VOCABULARY	The student uses advanced vocabulary with a high degree of accuracy.
4	ANSWER TO QUESTION	The student answers the question adequately but not thoroughly.
	COMPREHENSIBILITY	The student can generally be understood.
	ORGANIZATION	The student's response is adequately organized and developed.
	FLOW OF IDEAS	The student's ideas generally flow cohesively.
	GRAMMAR	The student uses either accurate easier grammatical structures or more advanced grammatical structures with a few errors.
	VOCABULARY	The student uses either accurate easier vocabulary or more advanced vocabulary with some errors.
3	ANSWER TO QUESTION	The student gives a basically accurate response to the question.
	COMPREHENSIBILITY	The student's basic ideas can be understood.
	ORGANIZATION	The student's response is organized basically and is not thoroughly developed.
	FLOW OF IDEAS	The student's ideas flow cohesively sometimes and at other times do not.
	GRAMMAR	The student has a number of errors in grammar or uses only very basic grammar fairly accurately.
	VOCABULARY	The student has a number of errors in vocabulary or uses only very basic vocabulary fairly accurately.

2	ANSWER TO QUESTION	The student discusses information from the task but does not answer the question directly.
	COMPREHENSIBILITY	The student's ideas are not always intelligible.
	ORGANIZATION	The student's response is not clearly organized and is incomplete or contains some inaccurate points.
	FLOW OF IDEAS	The student's ideas often do not flow cohesively.
	GRAMMAR	The student has numerous errors in grammar that interfere with meaning.
	VOCABULARY	The student has numerous errors in vocabulary that interfere with meaning.
1	ANSWER TO QUESTION	The student's response is only slightly related to the topic.
	COMPREHENSIBILITY	The student's ideas are occasionally intelligible.
	ORGANIZATION	The student's response is not clearly organized and is only minimally on the topic.
	FLOW OF IDEAS	The student's ideas do not flow smoothly.
	GRAMMAR	The student produces very little grammatically correct language.
	VOCABULARY	The student uses very little vocabulary correctly.
0	The student either writes nothing or fails to answer the question.	

The following chart shows how a score of 0 through 5 on a Writing task is converted to a scaled score out of 30.

WRITING SCORE (0–5)	WRITING SCALED SCORE (0–30)
5.00	30
4.75	29
4.50	28
4.25	27
4.00	25
3.75	24
3.50	22
3.25	21
3.00	20
2.75	18
2.50	17
2.25	15
2.00	14
1.75	12
1.50	11
1.25	10
1.00	8
0.75	7
0.50	5
0.25	4
0.00	0

Scaled scores on each of the Writing tasks on a test are averaged to determine the scaled score for the test.

RECORDING YOUR WRITING TEST RESULTS

Each time that you complete a Writing Pre-Test, Writing Post-Test, Writing Mini-Test, or Writing Complete Test, you should record the results in the chart that follows. In this way, you will be able to keep track of the progress you are making.

WRITING TEST RESULTS	
WRITING PRE-TEST	Writing Task 1 _____ Writing Task 2 _____ **Overall Writing Score** _____
WRITING POST-TEST	Writing Task 1 _____ Writing Task 2 _____ **Overall Writing Score** _____
WRITING MINI-TEST 1	Writing Task 1 _____ **Overall Writing Score** _____
WRITING MINI-TEST 2	Writing Task 1 _____ **Overall Writing Score** _____
WRITING MINI-TEST 3	Writing Task 1 _____ **Overall Writing Score** _____
WRITING MINI-TEST 4	Writing Task 1 _____ **Overall Writing Score** _____
WRITING MINI-TEST 5	Writing Task 1 _____ **Overall Writing Score** _____
WRITING MINI-TEST 6	Writing Task 1 _____ **Overall Writing Score** _____
WRITING MINI-TEST 7	Writing Task 1 _____ **Overall Writing Score** _____
WRITING MINI-TEST 8	Writing Task 1 _____ **Overall Writing Score** _____
WRITING COMPLETE TEST 1	Writing Task 1 _____ Writing Task 2 _____ **Overall Writing Score** _____
WRITING COMPLETE TEST 2	Writing Task 1 _____ Writing Task 2 _____ **Overall Writing Score** _____

RECORDING SCRIPT

WRITING DIAGNOSTIC PRE-TEST

Page 2

Question 1

Listen to the passage. On a piece of paper, take notes on the main points of the listening passage.

(professor) Now, I'd like to talk about the cause of childhood amnesia. Though its cause is not known for certain and various explanations have been hypothesized, one explanation is more generally accepted than others.

The generally accepted explanation for childhood amnesia has to do with a huge difference in the way that young children and adults encode their experiences. Young children simply encode their experiences randomly as they happen, while adults retain their memories in an organized way. Because a young child encodes events randomly, without forming associations between events or categorizing events in an organized way, the memories of the encoded events of young children don't last.

There are most likely numerous causes of the shift from early childhood random encoding to adult encoding in organized patterns. A major factor in this shift is the maturing of the hippocampus. . . . Do you know what the hippocampus is? H-I-P-P-O-C-A-M-P-U-S? It's a part of the brain; it's the part of the brain that helps organize and consolidate memories, and this part of the brain is not mature for at least the first two to three years of life. As a result, events that take place in the first two or three years can't be organized and consolidated and therefore most likely won't be remembered later in life.

HOW DOES THE INFORMATION IN THE LISTENING PASSAGE ADD TO THE IDEAS PRESENTED IN THE READING PASSAGE?

WRITING SKILLS

WRITING EXERCISE 2

Page 12

1. Listen to the passage. Take notes on the main points of the listening passage.

(professor) You've all read the passage on homeschooling? I'd like to discuss the ideas presented in the passage. I think some claims are made in the reading passage that are not completely true.

I've been a part of a state panel on homeschooling for the last ten years, so I'm pretty familiar with the issues surrounding homeschooling. I can tell you that a lot of people who are involved in homeschooling would disagree with the ideas in the article. Let me make a couple of points about what was in the reading passage.

First of all, it has not proven at all true that children with a homeschool education learn less than children in traditional schools. In fact, study after study has shown that children in homeschools learn far more than typical students in traditional schools.

The second point I'd like to make it that homeschooled children can have lots of opportunities for social interaction with other children. Parents who homeschool their children can arrange situations that involve social interaction with other homeschooled children. Thus, children who are homeschooled can have even more social interaction with other children than children in traditional schools because they can ineract with other children at any time of the day if their parents arrange this.

The final point I'd like to make is about variety in the curriculum in homeschools. Parents who homeschool their children can offer the broadest possible curriculum. Parents are not limited by school boards that decide on the curriculum in traditional schools. Parents may decide to teach astronomy, or medicine, or Chinese even if these subjects are not part of the curriculum in traditional schools.

Page 13

2. Listen to the passage. Take notes on the main points of the listening passage.

(professor) We've seen that polysemic words are words that have numerous meanings. Well, there is a really special group of polysemic words, and this special group consists of words that have not just different meanings but opposite meanings. Think about this, that there can be one word in English that has not just different meanings but meanings that are, in some sense, opposite.

Think about the words bolt and fast. If you bolt something, perhaps you bolt your door, then this means that it's locked fast, or fastened and cannot move or open. However, if someone decides to bolt, then he or she is running away, and running away very fast. So the word "bolt" can mean "locked and not moving" or conversely can mean "moving very quickly." The same can be said of the word "fast." This word can also mean "locked and not moving" or "moving very quickly."

Another interesting word of this type is the word *sanction*. Just think about what this word means. If you sanction something, it means that you permit it. However, if you put a sanction on something, then it means the opposite. In this case it means that you don't permit it.

OK, keep in mind that these words that you just learned about, "bolt," and "fast," and "sanction," are polysemic words because each can have different meanings. But they are special kinds of polysemic words because their meanings aren't simply different; their meanings are opposite in some sense.

Page 13

3. Listen to the passage. Take notes on the main points of the listening passage.

(*professor*) Now I'd like to talk about what some critics have to say about Margaret Mead's research. There is one very general criticism that comes out in critical reviews of Mead's work.

This general criticism of Mead's work is that what she saw in the three societies that she studied was just too pat, too neat, that it all fit too neatly into specific categories. She found these three societies that exhibited remarkably different gender roles, three societies that neatly fit into categories that she was looking to fill. It's not very normal for any society to have behavior that's so extreme, where one can say that all the people in the society act in the same extreme way. It's not very common, in anthropological research, in the study of human societies, that people fit very neatly into a limited number of categories because humans are far more complex than that.

Stated another way, this general criticism of Mead is that perhaps she was looking for societies that exhibit certain extreme behaviors as a whole, and when she found these three particular societies, she paid more attention to the behaviors that fit in with the theory she was trying to prove and perhaps did not pay enough attention to the behaviors that didn't fit into her theory.

WRITING REVIEW EXERCISE (Skills 1–8)

Page 29

Listen to the passage. On a piece of paper, take notes on the main points of the listening passage.

(*professor*) The reading passage discussed a common belief about Stonehenge, that Stonehenge was built by the Druids, the high priests of the Celts. Lots of people believe this today. I think, if you asked most people who built Stonehenge, they would say, "The Druids" or "The Celts." But this is clearly not true. Scientific tests today show that this isn't true. The dates just don't match up.

First, let me discuss what is known about when the Celts arrived in England. The Celts were flourishing on the European mainland, and they spread out from there to various places, including England. It's not quite clear when the Celts actually arrived in England; there are two different theories. One theory is that the Celts arrived in England around 1500 B.C., and the alternate theory is that the Celts started arriving in England around 800 B.C. In either case, the Celts were not in England before around 1500 B.C. There is universal agreement on that.

Now for the age of Stonehenge. Modern radiocarbon dating techniques have been used on Stonehenge to determine its age. Radiocarbon testing is a process used to date specimens by measuring the amount of carbon-14 remaining in them. Well, the radiocarbon testing has shown that Stonehenge was built in three phases. The first phase was around 3000 B.C., and the second phase was around 2800 B.C. The third phase, the phase when the giant stones actually went up, was around 2100 B.C.

You can see from the dates, no matter which theory you believe about the arrival of the Celts in England, that the Celts and their Druid priests had not yet arrived in England when Stonehenge was built and could not possibly be the culture that constructed Stonehenge.

HOW DOES THE INFORMATION IN THE LISTENING PASSAGE CAST DOUBT ON THE BELIEF IN THE READING PASSAGE?

WRITING POST-TEST

Page 51

Question 1

Listen to the passage. On a piece of paper, take notes on the main points of the listening passage.

(*professor*) Do you understand the concept of unintended consequences? That sometimes, when a decision is made, there are consequences of that decision that are unexpected? This, of course, can take place in any field, in any field where decisions are made, but we're going to look at this concept in terms of government decision-making.

Let's take, for example, a situation where a local government needed to increase revenue, so it decided to raise taxes. Makes sense, doesn't it, that the government should have raised taxes if it wanted to increase revenues?

Well, let's look at what happened in this situation. This government wanted to raise revenue, so it increased taxes, and, for a short while, tax revenue was higher. But then, guess what happened! The citizens of the area who were paying higher taxes had less money to spend, because they were paying higher taxes, you see. Well, because the citizens had less money to spend, they bought fewer goods. And what happened to companies when they were selling fewer goods? Well, they paid less in taxes, for one thing, and they had to lay off employees, for another. And these employees who lost their jobs paid no taxes because they weren't working, you see. So, look at the overall situation in this area after a few years. The local government had raised taxes to increase revenue; however, when the government raised taxes, revenue actually went down rather than up. That's an unexpected consequence.

HOW DOES THE INFORMATION IN THE LISTENING PASSAGE ADD TO THE IDEAS PRESENTED IN THE READING PASSAGE?

WRITING MINI-TEST 1

Page 55

Listen to the passage. On a piece of paper, take notes on the main points of the listening passage.

(professor) You may read all of this information about garlic, about how it was used in the past, and think that this was all just a lot of superstition, like breaking a mirror brings seven years of bad luck or throwing salt over your shoulder protects you from bad luck. But this is different. It's not all just superstition, though some of it is. There's actually a lot of scientific evidence that garlic does have certain medicinal benefits.

First of all, garlic does kill bacteria. In 1858, Louis Pasteur conducted some research that showed that garlic does actually kill bacteria. When garlic was used during World War I to prevent infection, there was good reason. There is actually research to back up garlic's ability to kill bacteria. It's raw, or

uncooked, garlic that has this property. Raw garlic has been shown to kill twenty-three different kinds of bacteria.

Then, when garlic is heated, it's been shown to have different medicinal properties. When it's heated, garlic forms a compound that thins the blood. The blood-thinning property can help prevent arteries from clogging and reduce blood pressure, which may have some impact on preventing heart attacks and strokes.

HOW DOES THE INFORMATION IN THE LISTENING PASSAGE SUPPORT THE INFORMATION PRESENTED IN THE READING PASSAGE?

WRITING MINI-TEST 3

Page 59

Listen to the passage. On a piece of paper, take notes on the main points of the listening passage.

(professor) Well, when managers tried out these principles of scientific management in their factories in the early twentieth century, things did not work out as expected. Many factory managers did not find the improved efficiency, lower costs, and higher profits they expected from scientific management. Instead, they often found the exact opposite.

The first problem managers ran into was with the time-and-motion studies. Very thorough time-and-motion studies were necessary to improve productivity, and very thorough time-and-motion studies were very costly, so they added to costs and did not improve profits. In addition, these time-and-motion studies were often difficult to conduct because the workers in the factory were so resistant to them.

In addition to the problem with the time-and-motion studies, there was also a problem with the lower-skilled workers. When the principles of scientific management are applied to lower-skilled workers, these lower-skilled workers must work like machines. They must change the way they work so that they work in exactly the same way as other workers, and they must do the same single repetitive motion over and over again, thousands of times a day. The low-skilled workers were not eager to work this way and often took steps to make the process less efficient.

Finally, there was also a serious problem with the high-skilled workers. One of the components of scientific management was to break down the jobs of higher-skilled workers into smaller tasks that lower-skilled workers could do, in order to save money. The result of this for the higher-skilled workers was that they would no longer have high-paying jobs. Thus, the higher-skilled workers were extremely resistant to attempts to institute scientific management.

Overall, managers who tried to employ the principles of scientific management found that they had lower efficiency, higher costs, and lower profits than they had expected.

HOW DO THE IDEAS IN THE LISTENING PASSAGE CAST DOUBT ON THE IDEAS IN THE READING PASSAGE?

WRITING MINI-TEST 5

Page 63

Listen to the passage. On a piece of paper, take notes on the main points of the listening passage.

(professor) Let me talk a bit about the expression "catch-22." Do you understand what a catch-22 is? This expression is so well known now that it has entered the American lexicon: well, a catch-22 is a situation that is unresolvable, one where there is no good choice, no best path to take.

In Heller's novel, the catch-22 is a very specific catch in a very specific situation. The situation in which the protagonist found himself was that he wanted to get out of combat by declaring himself insane. So you see that in this situation there was a very specific catch. In American culture now, though, this expression is used more generally. It refers to any situation where there's a catch, where there's no solution, where there's no way out.

One more bit of information about the expression "catch-22," about the number 22 in the expression. This number doesn't have any real meaning; it just signifies one in a long line of catches. Heller really could have used any number; it didn't have to be 22. When Heller was first writing the book, he used the number 14; the book was originally titled *Catch-14*. Then, in the production process, the number was changed to 18, so the title was *Catch-18*. But then there was a problem with the number 18 because there was another book with 18 in the title, so Heller's title became *Catch-22*.

HOW DOES THE INFORMATION IN THE LISTENING PASSAGE ADD TO THE IDEAS PRESENTED IN THE READING PASSAGE?

WRITING MINI-TEST 7

Page 67

Listen to the passage. On a piece of paper, take notes on the main points of the listening passage.

(professor) Type I Supernova, the kind of supernova that you read about in the reading passage, is not the only kind of supernova. The other kind of supernova is called, as you might expect, a Type II supernova.

A Type II supernova occurs when a large star, a single star and not a double star, is in the process of dying. A Type II supernova occurs only in a star that is truly massive, a star that is at least ten times as massive as our Sun.

A supernova occurs in this type of massive star only when it is very old. The core of such a massive star in its very late stages of life becomes progressively hotter and hotter until the core collapses and a whole series of thermonuclear reactions occur, causing a supernova.

Probably the most famous and brightest historical Type II supernova occurred in 1054, near the beginning of the last millennium. It was recorded in China, and Chinese records indicate that it was visible to the naked eye even during daylight for twenty-three days and was visible to the naked eye at night for 653 days, or almost two years. The Chinese also recorded two other supernovae, in 1006 and in 1181, though these were not as bright as the 1054 supernova. From then, it was not until 1987 that another Type II supernova was visible to the naked eye. In 1987, a Type II supernova occurred in a galaxy close to the Milky Way, our galaxy. This was the only supernova that was strong enough and close enough to Earth to be seen from Earth without a telescope in over 400 years, since the two Type I supernovae were observed in 1572 and 1604. The 1987 supernova was the only Type II supernova to be visible to the naked eye in close to a thousand years.

HOW DOES THE INFORMATION IN THE READING PASSAGE CONTRAST WITH THE INFORMATION IN THE LISTENING PASSAGE?

WRITING COMPLETE TEST 1

Page 71

Question 1

Listen to the passage. On a piece of paper, take notes on the main points of the listening passage.

(professor) It was really surprising to scientists when they found out that Venus was so hot because the clouds around Venus reflect almost all the light from the Sun back into space. The small amount of sunlight that's able to filter through the clouds doesn't seem like anywhere near enough light to make the temperature on Venus so high. Instead, because it's always so cloudy on the surface of Venus, the temperature should be rather cool.

You might think that the temperature on Venus is so hot because Venus is so close to the Sun, but this isn't really a good explanation for the heat on Venus. The temperature on Venus is even hotter than the temperature on Mercury, which is closer than Venus to the Sun, so the proximity of Venus to the Sun doesn't explain the high temperature on Venus.

Scientists are still not certain why the temperature on Venus is so high, but one possible explanation is Venus's carbon dioxide atmosphere. The very dense atmosphere on Venus is almost entirely carbon dioxide. This carbon dioxide may create a barrier that traps any heat that gets through beneath it and doesn't let it escape.

HOW DOES THE INFORMATION IN THE LISTENING PASSAGE ADD TO THE INFORMATION PRESENTED IN THE READING PASSAGE?

WRITING COMPLETE TEST 2

Page 74

Question 1

Listen to the passage. On a piece of paper, take notes on the main points of the listening passage.

(professor) Now I'd like to talk about results after the sixth grade testing program had been in effect in the Hamilton School District for ten years. Well, sadly, the school district was not pleased with the results. Ten years after instituting the program, the school district found the following to be true.

First of all, the school district found that social promotion had not ended in grades one through five. It was not until students had finished the sixth grade that they were tested. The test at the end of grade six identified which students were behind at that point and which students were prepared to move on. However, because the test showed that a number of students were really behind in the sixth grade, it was clear from this that these students had been behind in earlier grades but had been socially promoted. It seemed evident that the sixth grade test had not brought an end to social promotion in grades one through five.

Something else the district found to be true after ten years of sixth grade testing was that, by waiting until the sixth grade to test students, there were just as many unprepared students as there had been before the testing program was instituted and these students were really far behind. Students who had not been prepared in earlier grades had clearly been socially promoted for several years, so by waiting so long to test students, some students had gotten really far behind, just as many students as had been unprepared without the sixth grade testing.

A final conclusion that the district drew ten years after the implementation of sixth grade testing was that more students were dropping out and failing to graduate than before the implementation of the program. Far more students were being held back at the end of the six grade than had been held back before the implementation of the program, and many students had to be held back for more than one year to catch up enough to pass the sixth grade test. Since students who are held back tend to drop out at a really high rate, the percentage of students graduating from high school after the program was implemented was lower than the percentage of students graduating from high school before the program was implemented.

As a result of these unexpected and unacceptable outcomes from the program of sixth grade testing, the Hamilton School District decided to end the testing program after ten years.

HOW DO THE IDEAS IN THE LISTENING PASSAGE CHALLENGE THE IDEAS IN THE READING PASSAGE?

ANSWER KEY

WRITING DIAGNOSTIC PRE-TEST Page 1

Question 1 Page 2

Sample Notes

TOPIC OF READING PASSAGE: childhood amnesia, a phenomenon of human memory (inability to remember early years)

studies of childhood amnesia:
• difficult to test whether memories are accurate
• still show that people do not remember first 3 to 5 years

TOPIC OF LISTENING PASSAGE: why childhood amnesia occurs

possible cause of childhood amnesia:
• young children encode randomly (before hippocampus matures and helps to organize memories)
• adults encode in organized patterns (after hippocampus matures)

Sample Answer

In this set of materials, the reading passage discusses a certain phenomenon in human memory, and the listening passage adds to the ideas in the reading passage by presenting a possible explanation for this phenomenon.

The reading passage discusses childhood amnesia, which is the inability to remember one's early years. Studies on childhood amnesia show that it is difficult to test whether or not memories from childhood are accurate and that people basically do not remember their first three to five years.

The reading passage discusses a possible explanation for childhood amnesia. This explanation is that young children encode information before the hippocampus matures and adults encode information after the hippocampus matures. Because the hippocampus helps to organize memories, young children encode information randomly, while adults encode memories in an organized way. The fact that children encode information randomly would help to explain why childhood amnesia occurs.

WRITING SKILLS

WRITING EXERCISE 1 Page 8

Sample Notes

1. TOPIC OF READING PASSAGE: disadvantages of homeschooling

   main points about the topic:
   • less learning in homeschools than in traditional schools
   • less social interaction in homeschools than in traditional schools
   • less varied curriculum in homeschools than in traditional schools

2. TOPIC OF READING PASSAGE: polysemy (one word having different meanings)

   main points about the topic:
   • *sound* (19 noun meanings, 12 adjective meanings, 12 verb meanings, 4 meanings in verb phrases, 2 adverb meanings)
   • *set* (57 noun meanings, 120 verb meanings)

3. TOPIC OF READING PASSAGE: Margaret Mead's studies of three societies in New Guinea

   main points about the topic:
   • first society = both men and women have "feminine" characteristics
   • second society = both men and women have "masculine" characteristics
   • third society = men have "feminine" characteristics, women have "masculine" characteristics
   • conclusion = gender characteristics come more from society than from biology

WRITING EXERCISE 2 Page 12

Sample Notes

1. TOPIC OF LISTENING PASSAGE: advantages of homeschooling

   main points about the topic:
   • more learning possible in homeschools
   • more social interaction possible in homeschools
   • varied curriculum possible in homeschools

2. TOPIC OF LISTENING PASSAGE: special subset of polysemic words (one word with opposite meanings)

   main points about the topic: examples of words with opposite meanings
   • "bolt" and "fast" (meaning "cannot move" or "move quickly")
   • "sanction" (meaning "permit" or "not permit")

3. TOPIC OF LISTENING PASSAGE: criticisms of Mead's research

   main points about the topic: criticisms
   • results "too neat" (research not usually this tidy)
   • results suggest Mead found what she was looking for rather than what was there

WRITING EXERCISE 3 Page 16

1. reading passage describes *disadvantages*; listening passage describes advantages

2. reading passage describes a *category of words*; listening passage describes *subset of category*

3. reading passage describes *research*; listening passage describes *criticisms of the research*

WRITING EXERCISE 4 Page 19

1. TOPIC STATEMENT: In this set of materials, the reading passage discusses several disadvantages of homeschooling. The listening passage challenges the ideas in the reading passage by listing advantages of homeschooling.

2. TOPIC STATEMENT: In this set of materials, the reading passage describes a certain category of words, and the listening passage adds to this information by describing a special subset of words in this category.

3. TOPIC STATEMENT In this set of materials, the reading passage describes research by Margaret Mead, and the listening passage casts doubt on this research by offering some criticisms of it.

WRITING EXERCISE 5 Page 21

1. The reading passage discusses advantages of homeschooling. It states that there is less learning, less social interaction, and less variety in the curriculum in homeschools than there is in traditional schools.

2. The reading passage defines "polysemy" and provides two examples of it. Polysemy exists when one word has different meanings. The word "sound" has 19 noun meanings, 12 adjective meanings, 12 verb meanings, 4 meanings in verb phrases, and 2 adverb meanings. The word "set" has 57 noun meanings and 120 verb meanings.

3. The reading passage discusses Margaret Mead's research on culture and gender roles in three cultures. In the first culture, both men and woman have "feminine" characteristics; in the second culture, both men and women have "masculine" characteristics; in the third culture, men have "feminine" characteristics, and women have "masculine" characteristics. From this, Mead came to the conclusion that gender characteristics come more from society than from biology.

WRITING EXERCISE 6 Page 24

1. The listening passage casts doubt on the reading passage by saying that the advantages listed in the reading passage are not correct. According to the listening passage, students in homeschools can learn more, can have more social interaction, and can have a wider variety in the curriculum than students in traditional schools. This directly contradicts the reading passage, which says that students in homeschools learn less, have less social interaction, and have a narrower curriculum than students in traditional schools.

2. The listening passage describes a special subset of polysemic words. This special subset is words whose meanings are not just different; the meanings are opposite. Three examples of this subset of polysemic words are provided. "Bolt" and "fast" can each have meanings of "cannot move" or "move quickly," and "sanction" can mean either "permit" or "not permit."

3. The listening passage casts doubt on Mead's conclusion by listing two different criticisms of Mead's research. The first criticism was that Mead's results were "too neat" in that she researched three cultures and found three really specific and contrasting situations; it was "too neat" because research is not usually this tidy. The second criticism was that the results suggest that Mead found what she was looking for rather than what was there; she was looking for really different gender roles in different cultures, and this is exactly what she found.

WRITING EXERCISE 7 Page 26

1. (A) In this set of materials, the reading passage discusses one type of management **style, and the** listening passage presents the opposite type of management style. Both of the management **styles were** proposed by Douglas McGregor.
(B) The reading passage discusses the theory X management style, **which is an** authoritarian management style. What a theory X manager **believes is** that employees dislike work and will try to avoid it. Since this type of manager believes that employees do not like to **work, he** or she must force employees to **work. A** manager must force employees to work with threats and punishment.
(C) The listening passage discusses a very different management **style; it** discusses the theory Y management style, which is a participative style of management. A theory Y manager believes that employees **work** for enjoyment. Employees do not need to be **threatened; they** work for the pleasure of working. The role that this type of manager needs to **follow is** to set objectives and then to reward **employees as** they meet these objectives.

2. (A) In this set of materials, the reading passage describes the different types of waves that occur during **earthquakes, and** the listening passage explains how much damage each of these types of waves **causes.**
(B) According to the reading passage, three different types of **waves occur** during an earthquake: primary (or P) waves, secondary (or S) waves, and surface waves. Primary waves are the fastest-moving **waves, and secondary** waves are not as fast as primary waves. Surface waves resemble the ripples in a pond after a stone has been thrown in **it; they** are very slow-moving waves.
(C) According to the listening passage, the types of waves that occur during an **earthquake do** not cause equal amounts of damage to structures. What causes most damage to structures during **earthquakes is** surface waves. The really slow-moving surface waves cause most of the differential movement of buildings during earthquakes, **and it is** the differential movement of buildings that causes most of the damage. Because the primary and secondary waves vibrate much faster and with less movement than surface **waves, they** cause little damage to structures.

WRITING EXERCISE 8 Page 27

1. (A) In this set of materials, the reading passage discusses **an attempt** to deal with the problem of spelling in **many** words in American English; the listening passage **explains** why this attempt was not a **successful** one.
(B) The reading passage explains that there is a problem in spelling a number of **words** in English where the spelling and pronunciation **do** not match; it then goes on to explain that philanthropist Andrew

Carnegie made **an effort** to resolve this. He gave **a huge** amount of **money** to establish a board **called** the Simplified Spelling Board. As the name of **the board** indicates, **its** purpose was to simplify the spellings **of words** that are difficult to spell in English. Because of all **of the work** that the board did, spellings like *ax* (instead of *axe*) and *program* (instead of *programme*) **became** acceptable in American English.

(C) The listening passage **explains** why the work of the Simplified Spelling Board **did** not last. According to the listening passage, the main reason for the board's problems **was** that it went too far. **It** tried to establish spellings like *yu* (instead of *you*) and *tuff* (instead of *tough*). There was a **really** negative reaction to the attempt to change spelling too much, and eventually the board was **dissolved**.

2. (A) In this set of materials, the reading passage describes **a type** of learning, and the listening passage **provides** an **extended** example of this type of learning.

(B) The reading passage discusses aversive conditioning, which is **defined** as learning involving an unpleasant stimulus. In this type of learning, an unpleasant stimulus is **applied** every **time** that a certain behavior occurs, in an attempt to stop the behavior. A learner **can behave** in two different **ways** in response to the knowledge that something unpleasant will soon **occur**. Avoidance behavior is **a change** in behavior before the stimulus **is** applied to avoid the unpleasant stimulus, while escape behavior is the opposite, a change in behavior after the application of the stimulus to cause **it** to stop.

(C) The listening passage provides **a long** example of aversive conditioning. This extended example is about the alarm in **many** cars that **buzzes** if the driver's seat belt is not fastened. In this example, the method of aversive conditioning that is applied to drivers **is** that every time a driver tries to drive with the seat belt unfastened, the buzzer **goes** off. The driver exhibits avoidance behavior if he or she **fastens** the seat belt before driving, to avoid hearing the buzzer. The driver exhibits escape behavior if he or she **attaches** the seat belt after the alarm **has started** to buzz, to stop the buzzing.

WRITING REVIEW EXERCISE (Skills 1–8) Page 29

Sample Notes

TOPIC OF READING PASSAGE: belief about the construction of Stonehenge (huge stone structure on Salisbury Plain in England)

main points about the topic:
- common belief that Stonehenge was built by Druids (high priests of Celts)
- chapter in book by John Aubrey (1626–1697) supporting Druids as builders of Stonehenge
- scholarly work by Dr. William Stukeley (1687–1765) supporting Druids as builders of Stonehenge

TOPIC OF LISTENING PASSAGE: impossibility of belief about Stonehenge (that Druids built it) because of the dates

main points about the topic:
- arrival of Celts and Druids in England (in 1500 B.C. or 800 B.C.)
- construction of Stonehenge in three phases (3000 B.C., 2800 B.C., 2100 B.C.)

Sample Answer

In this set of materials, the reading passage discusses a belief, and the listening passage casts doubt on this belief by showing that it is impossible because of the dates that events happened.

The reading passage discusses the belief that Stonehenge, a huge stone structure on Salisbury Plain in England, was built by the Druids, who were the high priests of the Celtic culture. Two works that support this belief are a chapter in a book by John Aubrey (1626–1697) and a scholarly work by Dr. William Stukeley (1687–1765).

The listening passage casts doubt on the belief in the reading passage by showing that the dates of certain events make it impossible. First, the listening passage indicates that the Celts and Druids arrived in England in either 1500 B.C. or 800 B.C. Then, the listening passage indicates that scientific studies show that Stonehenge was constructed in three phases, starting in 3000 B.C. and ending in 2100 B.C. If Stonehenge was finished in 2100 B.C. and the Celts and Druids did not arrive in England until 1500 B.C. at the earliest, then the belief expressed in the reading passage, that the Celts and Druids built Stonehenge, could not be true.

WRITING EXERCISE 11 Page 40

1. 3
2. 4
3. mysterious-sounding answer
4. I do not know.
5. amazed
6. English
7. assignment
8. classmate
9. 3 (this language, this expression, this mysterious-sounding answer)
10. 1 (these two examples)
11. For instance
12. an even more interesting example
13. Overall

WRITING EXERCISE 14 Page 48

(A) I definitely believe that taking part in organized team sports is beneficial. However, **it is** beneficial for much more than the obvious reasons. Everyone recognizes, of course, that participation in sports provides obvious physical benefits. It **leads** to improved physical **fitness; it** also provides a release from the stresses of life. I spent my youth taking part in a number of organized sports, including football, basketball, and **volleyball; as** a result of this experience I understand that the benefits of **participation are much** greater than the physical benefits.

(B) One very valuable benefit that children get from taking part in **sports is** that it teaches participants teamwork. What any player in a team sport needs to **learn is** that individual team members must put the team ahead of individual achievement. Individuals on one team who are working for individual glory rather than the good of the **team often** end up working against each other. A team made up of individuals unable to work **together is often** not a very successful **team; it** is usually a complete failure.

(C)   What also makes participation in team sports **valuable is** that it teaches participants to work to achieve goals. Playing **sports involves** setting goals and working toward **them; examples** of such goals are running faster, kicking harder, throwing straighter, or jumping higher. Athletes learn **that they can** set goals and work toward them until the **goals are accomplished. It is** through hard work that goals can be met.

(D)   By taking part in **sports, one can** learn the truly valuable skills of working together on teams and working to accomplish specific goals. These **goals are not** just beneficial in **sports; more** importantly, the skills that are developed through **sports are** the basis of success in many other aspects of life. Mastering these skills **leads** to success not only on the playing field but also in the wider arena of life.

WRITING EXERCISE 15   Page 50

(A)   In my first semester at the university, I was **overwhelmed** by the differences between university studies and high school studies. In high school, I had easily **been** able to finish the **amount** of work that was assigned, and if **on a certain** occasion I did not complete an assignment, the teacher quickly **told** me to make up the work. The situation in my university classes **was** not at all like the situation in high school.

(B)   I was tremendously **surprised** at the volume of work assigned in the university. Unlike high school courses, which perhaps covered a chapter in two **weeks**, university courses **regularly** covered two or three chapters in one week and two or three other chapters in the next week. I **had** been able to keep up with the workload in high school, but it was difficult for me to finish all the reading in **my** university classes even though I tried **really** hard to finish all of **it**.

(C)   The role that the teacher took in motivating students to get work done **was** also very different in my university. In high school, if an assignment was **unfinished** on **the** date that it was due, my teacher would **immediately** let me know that I had **really made** a mistake and needed to finish **the** assignment right away. In my university classes, however, professors did not **regularly inform** students to make sure that we were **getting** work done on schedule. It was really easy to put off studying in the beginning of each **semester** and really have to work hard later in the semester to catch up on my assignments.

(D)   During my first year in the university, I had to **set a firm** goal to get things done by myself instead of relying on others to watch over me and make sure that I **had** done what I was supposed to do. With so **many** assignments, this was quite a **difficult task**, but I now **regularly** try to do my best because I dislike being very far behind. It seems that I have **turned** into quite a **motivated** student.

WRITING POST-TEST   Page 51

Question 1   Page 52

Sample Notes

TOPIC OF READING PASSAGE: unintended consequences (effects that are unexpected after a decision)

example of parking ban on Main Street:
- positive consequence = some people get more exercise walking
- negative consequence = some people stop shopping in stores on Main Street

TOPIC OF LISTENING PASSAGE: extended example of unintended consequences

example of increased taxes:
- local government raised taxes to increase revenue
- decision ended up decreasing revenue (citizens had less to spend because of increased taxes)

Sample Answer

In this set of materials, the reading passage defines a concept and provides a brief example of the concept. The listening passage adds to the ideas in the reading passage by providing a more extended example of the concept.

The reading passage discusses the concept of unintended consequences, which is about the effects that are unexpected after a decision. A brief example is given in which a parking ban is instituted on Main Street. There are positive unintended consequences when some people get more exercise walking, and there are negative unintended consequences when some people stop shopping in stores on Main Street.

The listening passage provides a more extended example of unintended consequences from the field of economics. This extended example deals with the unintended consequences of an increase in taxes. In raising taxes, the local government expected to increase revenue. However, where taxes were raised, citizens had less to spend because of the increased taxes, and the decision ended up decreasing revenue instead of the expected increase. Just as there were unintended consequences in the decision to ban parking on Main Street, the decision to increase taxes in order to increase revenue also had the very unintended consequence of lowering revenue.

WRITING MINI-TEST 1   Page 54

Sample Notes   Page 55

TOPIC OF READING PASSAGE: uses of garlic throughout history

how garlic has been used:
- Egyptians (to cure 22 ailments and make workers stronger)
- Greeks and Romans (to cure illnesses, ward off spells and curses, make soldiers courageous)
- Homer, Vikings, Marco Polo (to help during long voyages)
- World War I (to fight infections)

TOPIC OF LISTENING PASSAGE: scientific evidence showing benefits of garlic

evidence of benefits:
- raw garlic (kills 23 kinds of bacteria)
- heated garlic (thins blood)

Sample Answer

In this set of materials, the reading passage describes various uses of garlic, and the listening passage supports the ideas in the reading passage by providing evidence that proves garlic's benefits.

The reading passage describes how garlic has been used throughout history. The Egyptians used garlic to cure 22 ailments and to make workers stronger. The Greeks and Romans used garlic to cure illnesses, to ward off spells and curses, and to make soldiers courageous. Homer, the Vikings, and Marco Polo used garlic to help during long voyages, and garlic was used in World War I to fight infections.

The listening passage cites scientific evidence showing that garlic does have benefits. The evidence shows that raw garlic kills 23 kinds of bacteria and that heated garlic thins the blood. This means that at least some of the ways that garlic was used throughout history may have been truly effective.

WRITING MINI-TEST 3   Page 58

Sample Notes   Page 59

TOPIC OF READING PASSAGE: scientific management in theory
- thorough time-and-motion studies conducted
- low-skilled workers trained to improve performance
- high-skilled workers replaced by low-skilled workers
- improved efficiency, lower costs, greater profits achieved

TOPIC OF LISTENING PASSAGE: scientific management in practice
- high cost of time-and-motion studies
- low-skilled workers unwilling to play the assigned mechanical role
- high-skilled workers resistant to losing jobs
- lower efficiency, higher costs, lower profits achieved

Sample Answer

In this set of materials, the reading passage discusses a theory, and the listening passage casts doubt on the effectiveness of the theory by showing what happens when the theory was put into practice.

The reading passage discusses the theory of scientific management. According to this theory thorough time-and-motion studies need to be conducted in factories so that low-skilled workers can be trained to improve performance and high-skilled workers can be replaced by low-skilled workers. In this way, there can be improved efficiency, lower costs, and greater profits in factories.

The listening passage casts doubt on this theory by showing what actually happened when managers tried to use this theory in their factories. When managers tried to use scientific management in their factories, they found that the necessary time-and-motion studies cost a lot, adding to the cost of running the factory. They also found that it was not easy to get the low-skilled workers to change the way they did their jobs because they were unwilling to act like machines in doing their jobs. Finally, they found that high-skilled workers were resistant to losing their jobs, so they were unhelpful in implementing scientific management. Overall, managers did not find the improved efficiency, lower costs, and greater profits that they expected from the theory; instead they found that efficiency was lower, costs were higher, and profits were lower.

WRITING MINI-TEST 5   Page 62

Sample Notes   Page 63

TOPIC OF READING PASSAGE: Joseph Heller's novel *Catch-22*

what the novel is about:
- takes place during World War II
- features bombardier who does not want to be in war

how the novel achieved success:
- book was originally not successful
- during later war, book became very successful

TOPIC OF LISTENING PASSAGE: significance of title *Catch-22*

significance of title:
- title refers to situation with no good choice
- phrase now part of American culture
- number 22 has no special meaning (could be different number)

Sample Answer

In this set of materials, the reading passage describes the novel *Catch-22*, and the listening passage adds to this information by explaining the significance of the title of the novel.

The reading describes what the novel *Catch-22* is about and how the novel achieved success. The novel takes place during World War II, and it features a bombardier who does not want to be in the war. It was originally not successful, but during a later war it became very successful.

The listening passage adds to this information by explaining the significance of the unusual title, *Catch-22*. According to the listening passage, the title refers to a situation with no good choice, and the phrase "catch-22" is now a part of American culture. The number *22* in the title actually had no specific significance to the author; any number could have been used in the title.

WRITING MINI-TEST 7   Page 66

Sample Notes   Page 67

TOPIC OF READING PASSAGE: Type I kind of supernova

main points about the topic:
- occurs in double star (white dwarf and companion star)

- occurs when companion grows and matter from it flows to white dwarf (until mass is 1.4 times that of Sun)
- two visible in recorded history (1572 and 1604)

TOPIC OF LISTENING PASSAGE: Type II kind of supernova

main points about the topic:

- occurs in a massive single star (ten times as big as Sun)
- occurs when massive star becomes hot enough to explode
- four visible in last millennium (1006, 1054, 1181, and 1987)

Sample Answer

In this set of materials, the reading passage describes one kind of supernova, and the listening passage presents a contrasting kind of supernova.

The reading passage describes a Type I supernova. According to the reading passage, a Type I supernova occurs in a double star, which is made up of a white dwarf and a companion star. The supernova occurs in a double star when the companion star grows and matter from it flows to the white dwarf. Only two visible Type I supernovas have occurred in recorded history, in 1572 and in 1604.

The listening passage describes a Type II supernova, which is quite different from the Type I supernova that was described in the reading passage. While a Type I supernova occurs in a double star, when material from the companion star flows to the white dwarf in the double star, a Type II supernova occurs in a massive single star. A Type II supernova occurs when a massive single star, one that is ten times as big as our Sun, becomes so hot that it explodes; this is much larger than a white dwarf, which explodes in a supernova when it is 1.4 times the mass of the Sun. Only one visible Type II supernova has occurred since the 12th century, so neither Type II nor Type I supernovas that are visible to the naked eye are very common.

WRITING COMPLETE TEST 1 Page 70

Question 1 Page 71

Sample Notes

TOPIC OF READING PASSAGE: characteristics of planet Venus

characteristics:

- shines brightly (so is called Morning Star and Evening Star)
- covered with clouds (clouds reflect sunlight)
- extremely hot (around 900 degrees Fahrenheit)

TOPIC OF LISTENING PASSAGE: surprising heat on Venus

what is surprising about heat:

- clouds reflect sunlight away from Venus
- Venus is farther away from Sun than Mercury but is hotter than Mercury

possible explanation for heat:

- dense atmosphere made of carbon dioxide
- heat trapped by dense atmosphere

Sample Answer

In this set of materials, the reading passage discusses certain characteristics of Venus, and the listening passage provides a possible explanation for one of these surprising characteristics.

Three notable characteristics of Venus are described in the reading passage. The first characteristic is that Venus shines so brightly that it is called the Morning Star and the Evening Star because it is visible in the morning and evening from Earth. The second characteristic that is discussed in the reading passage is the fact that Venus is covered with clouds that reflect sunlight. The third characteristic is that Venus is extremely hot, around 900 degrees Fahrenheit.

The listening passage adds to the reading passage by providing further explanation about the third characteristic, the extremely high heat on Venus. The heat is surprising because the thick clouds surrounding Venus reflect sunlight away from Venus and because Venus is father away from the Sun than Mercury but is hotter than Mercury. A possible explanation for the heat is that perhaps the dense atmosphere of carbon dioxide traps heat and does not allow it to escape.

WRITING COMPLETE TEST 2 Page 73

Question 1 Page 74

Sample Answer

In this set of materials, the reading passage discusses a program instituted in a certain school, and the listening passage describes the actual outcomes of the program.

The reading passage discusses a testing program instituted by Hamilton School District. The school district decided to test all sixth graders to determine whether or not they could go on to junior high school. Through this program, the district hoped to end social promotion, to have more well-prepared students, and to have a higher graduation rate.

The listening passage shows that the program did not turn out the way that the school district had expected. The district had hoped to end social promotion, but after the program had been in existence for ten years, there was clearly no end to social promotion. Next, the district had hoped that there would be more well-prepared students, but there were not more well-prepared students because the same number had clearly been socially promoted for the first five years. Finally, the district had hoped that the percentage of students graduating would be higher, but the opposite was true. The percentage of students graduating was actually lower because more students were held back and students who are held back drop out more often.

APPENDIX A Page 76

APPENDIX EXERCISE A1 Page 77

1. *pleases; chance*
2. *speaks; energy*
3. *competitor; shocked; outcome*
4. *remarks; brief*
5. *problems; resolved*
6. *acts; positive; determined*
7. *indicated; finish; eventually*
8. *answers; succinct*
9. *complex; explanation*
10. *novel; concept*
11. *appreciates; animated; discussions*
12. *reasons; involved; episode*

APPENDIX EXERCISE A2 Page 79

1. *this; herself; she; them; her; this*
2. *our; ourselves; your; mine; our; we; it; ourselves; this*
3. *these; they; their; them; themselves; they; themselves*
4. *he; this; he; it; him; his; himself; he; his*

APPENDIX EXERCISE A3 Page 81

1. *However*
2. *For instance*
3. *Furthermore*
4. *In fact*
5. *Fortunately*
6. *in contrast*
7. *nonetheless*
8. *therefore*
9. *moreover*
10. *in summary*
11. *surprisingly*
12. *on the other hand*
13. *for example*
14. *as a result*
15. *in conclusion*
16. *consequently*
17. *in addition*
18. *nevertheless*
19. *interestingly*
20. *indeed*

APPENDIX REVIEW EXERCISE (A1–A3) Page 82

1. It (B); he (B); His (B); fear (A); act (A)
2. it (B); However (C); agreement (A); this (B); main (A); point (A); board (A)
3. her (B); lecture (A); these (B); concepts (A)
4. He (B); objected (A); Nonetheless (C); plan (A)
5. no late (A); assignments (A); In fact (C); assignment (A); submitted (A); on time (A)
6. Unfortunately (C); this (B); account (A); newspaper (A); these (B); inaccuracies (A)
7. you (B); this (B); decision (A); yourself (B); Choosing (A); thesis (A); comprehensive exam (A); decision (A)
8. Indeed (C); outset (A); huge amount of effort (A); project (A); Not surprisingly (C); their (B); effort (A); they (B); project (A)
9. However (C); assignment (A); professor (A); assignment (A); he (B); These (B); contradictory things (A); students (A); confused (A)
10. these (B); corporations (A); students (A); interviews (A); campus (A); corporate (A); representatives (A); campus (A); interviews (A); Thus (C); sign up (A); interviews (A)

APPENDIX B Page 84

APPENDIX EXERCISE B1 Page 85

I 1. reasons
I 2. (When) everyone . . . decided
C 3. I found
I 4. discusses
I 5. preference
C 6. piece . . . was found
I 7. (As soon as) . . . article . . . appears
I 8. is
I 9. agreement
C 10. It happened
I 11. (As) no one . . . would have made
I 12. made
C 13. agreement . . . has been reached
I 14. poem
I 15. (Now that) you have told
C 16. We forgot
I 17.
I 18. (If) you think
C 19. manager . . . made
I 20. (Even though) you gave

APPENDIX EXERCISE B2 Page 87

I 1. matter was . . . (,) I could to decide
C 2. children broke . . . (, but) . . . parents did . . . find out
I 3. She expected . . . (, however) she did . . . graduate
C 4. family moved . . . (; as a result,) I . . . had
I 5. I made . . . (and) I vowed
C 6. Sam did . . . sign . . . (, so) he signed
C 7. students waited . . . (. Finally,) they got
I 8. parents advised . . . ( ) he did . . . take
I 9. job . . . was . . . (,) . . . I was given
C 10. Tom . . . wanted . . . (, yet) he did . . . know
I 11. We must return . . . (, otherwise) we will have
C 12. She . . . tries . . . (. However,) she . . . loses
I 13. (Therefore) she has gotten . . . (,) she can pay
C 14. She had . . . (; as a result,) she is
I 15. They left . . . (,) it began
C 16. I wanted . . . (; unfortunately,) this was
C 17. I will have . . . (, or) I will . . . be
I 18. accident happened . . . (, afterwards,) . . . police came . . . wrote
I 19. plan has . . . ( ) it . . . has
C 20. directions must be followed . . . (; otherwise,) . . . outcome will be

APPENDIX EXERCISE B3 Page 89

I 1. reason (that) he took . . . it was
C 2. (Why) . . . man did . . . will . . . be
C 3. ticket (that) I needed . . . was
I 4. (What) . . . lifeguard did it was
I 5. day (when) I found . . . it was
C 6. teacher (whose) . . . I remember . . . was
I 7. (Where) we went . . . it was
I 8. (That) he . . . said . . . it could . . . be refuted
I 9. man (who) helped . . . he was
C 10. (How) . . . paper got . . . remains
I 11. (What) caused . . . it is
C 12. plans (that) we made . . . were
I 13. process . . . (which) . . . decisions were made it was
C 14. (Whatever) she gets is (what) she deserves
C 15. employee (who) has . . . (that) you need is

I 16. (What) he wrote . . . it could . . . be taken
I 17. officer (who) stopped . . . he gave
C 18. (How) he could believe . . . (that) is . . . is
C 19. reason (that) I applied . . . was (that) . . . tuition was
I 20. (Why) they said (what) they said . . . (who) tried . . . it was

APPENDIX REVIEW EXERCISE (B1–B3) Page 90

(possible corrections)

1. *relationships, the*	should be	*relationships; the*
2. *reached but*	should be	*reached, but*
o'clock, that	should be	*o'clock; that*
3. *morning it was*	should be	*morning was*
Friday it would	should be	*Friday would*
because did	should be	*because I did*
4. *scholarship have*	should be	*scholarships have*
5. *moves, it*	should be	*moves, but it*
career, so we	should be	*career, we*
6. (no errors)		
7. *raised, however*	should be	*raised; however*
8. *confidential, they*	should be	*confidential; they*
If want	should be	*If you want*
do it is	should be	*do is*
9. *trees and*	should be	*trees, and*
heard they would	should be	*heard would*
10. (no errors)		

APPENDIX C Page 91

APPENDIX EXERCISE C1 Page 92

C 1. rangers (in the eastern section) (of the park) have spotted
I 2. flowers (on the plum tree) (in the garden) has started
   (flowers . . . have started)
I 3. cost (of the books) (for all) (of his classes) are
   (cost . . . is)
C 4. reports . . . (by the staff) (for the manager) contain
I 5. light (from the candles) (on the end tables) provide
   (light . . . provides)
I 6. ideas . . . (at the meeting) (of the council) was
   (ideas . . . were)
C 7. gemstones (in the necklace) . . . (by the actress) were
I 8. speech (on a variety) (of topics) (of great importance) (to the citizens) are being broadcast
   (speech . . . is being broadcast)
C 9. tires (for the front) (of the car) are being installed
I 10. exams . . . (for the last week) (of the semester) is going
   (exams . . . are going)

APPENDIX EXERCISE C2 Page 93

C 1. All . . . (experience) has contributed
I 2. Most . . . (dishes) . . . was
   (Most . . . dishes . . . were)
I 3. Some . . . (details) . . . requires
   (Some . . . details . . . require)
C 4. Half . . . (material) needs
I 5. All . . . (homes) . . . was
   (All . . . homes . . . were)
I 6. Most . . . (children) . . . has improved
   (Most . . . children . . . have improved)

C 7. Some . . . (money) . . . has
I 8. half . . . (eggs) . . . was
   (half . . . eggs . . . were)
C 9. all . . . (medicine) has
C 10. most . . . (time) . . . was

APPENDIX EXERCISE C3 Page 95

I 1. was really scary (but) was still quite pleasure
   (pleasurable)
C 2. that he was sorry (and) that he would make amends
I 3. idealism, integrity, (and) dedicate
   (dedication)
I 4. tall (yet) . . . athlete
   (athletic)
C 5. call . . . , write . . . , (or) send
C 6. in the spring semester (but) not in the fall semester
I 7. back (and) forth . . . Los Angeles (and) New York . . . pick up . . . (and) delivers
   (deliver)
I 8. work . . . (or) studies
   (study)
C 9. pain, anger, resentment, frustration, (and) disbelief
C 10. well-rehearsed (yet) natural-sounding

APPENDIX EXERCISE C4 Page 96

I 1. (not only) plays football (but also) baseball
   (plays baseball)
C 2. (either) praised (or) scolded
I 3. (both) in the refrigerator (and) the freezer
   (in the freezer)
I 4. (neither) what you prefer (or) what I prefer
   (nor)
C 5. (not only) misplaced . . . (but also) couldn't find
I 6. (Either) you can work . . . (or) join
   (, or you can join)
C 7. She was (both) challenged by (and) frustrated with
C 8. (Neither) the manager (nor) any members
I 9. (either) register for three courses (or) for four courses
   (register for four courses)
I 10. (Both) the children (as well as) the baby-sitter
   (and)

APPENDIX EXERCISE C5 Page 97

I 1. (the unusualest)
   (the most unusual)
C 2. (more expensive than)
C 3. (the angriest)
I 4. (the hotter than)
   (hotter than)
I 5. (more cloudier) today (than)
   (cloudier . . . than)
C 6. (the most ancient)
C 7. (wider than)
I 8. (the most tallest)
   (the tallest)
I 9. (most efficient)
   (the most efficient)
C 10. (stronger) . . . (more flavorful than)

APPENDIX EXERCISE C6 Page 98

C 1. (the friendliest)
I 2. (the most difficult of)
   (more difficult than)

I 3. (a nicest disposition than)
   (a nicer disposition than)
C 4. (the best party)
I 5. (the most fuel-efficient of)
   (more fuel-efficient than)
I 6. (the drier that)
   (the driest that)
C 7. (the most understanding of)
I 8. (earlier that)
   (the earliest that)
I 9. (the highest of)
   (higher than)
C 10. (more reticent than)

APPENDIX REVIEW EXERCISE (C1–C6) `Page 99`

C 1.
C 2.
I 3. *(the nearest)*
I 4. *(left)*
I 5. *(were)*
I 6. *(the most important)*
C 7.
C 8.
I 9. *(a more honorable)*
C 10.
I 11. *(are)*
I 12. *(the most ridiculous)*
C 13.
I 14. *(were)*
C 15.

APPENDIX EXERCISE C7 `Page 100`

I 1. have came
   (have come)
C 2. thought . . . had told
I 3. has wore
   (has worn)
C 4. have blown
I 5. has running
   (has run)
C 6. had struck . . . had knocked
I 7. have drew
   (have drawn)
C 8. has taught
I 9. had . . . knew
   (had . . . known)
C 10. have . . . gotten

APPENDIX EXERCISE C8 `Page 101`

I 1. will be inaugurate
   (will be inaugurated)
C 2. were presented . . . are unchanged
I 3. was took
   (was taken)
C 4. has been promoted
I 5. are . . . arguing . . . is happens
   (is happening)
I 6. should . . . have been smoke . . . was
   (should . . . have been smoking)
C 7. was ringing
I 8. were froze
   (were frozen)
C 9. is wondering . . . will be departing
I 10. were take off . . . land
   (were taking off . . . landing)

APPENDIX EXERCISE C9 `Page 102`

(possible answers)

C 1. cannot return
I 2. may preferring
   (may prefer)
I 3. will depends
   (will depend)
C 4. might be coming
I 5. must to try
   (must try)
I 6. could taken
   (could take)
C 7. might announce
I 8. must . . . gave
   (must . . . give)
I 9. will going
   (will go or will be going)
C 10. was . . . would not start

APPENDIX EXERCISE C10 `Page 103`

I 1. need . . . was
   (need . . . is or needed . . . was)
C 2. has . . . describes . . . happened
I 3. told . . . is pleased . . . heard
   (was)
C 4. is . . . did . . . understand
C 5. had . . . is going
I 6. leaves . . . took
   (leaves . . . takes or left . . . took)
I 7. was landing . . . remain
   (was landing . . . remained or is landing . . . remain)
C 8. are . . . committed
I 9. filled . . . up . . . heads
   (headed)
C 10. understand . . . happened . . . are . . . occurred

APPENDIX EXERCISE C11 `Page 105`

(possible answers)

C 1. is . . . has graduated
I 2. had rung . . . leave
   (had rung . . . left or has rung . . . leave)
I 3. have visited . . . traveled
   (travel or have traveled)
C 4. found . . . had made
C 5. are based . . . have done
I 6. had been collected . . . dismisses
   (dismissed)
C 7. was . . . growing . . . had . . . been
C 8. knows . . . have . . . tried
C 9. can tell . . . know . . . has transpired
C 10. will be . . . have submitted

APPENDIX EXERCISE C12 `Page 106`

I 1. (By 1995) . . . has decided
   (had decided)
C 2. was established (in 1900)
I 3. (Since) . . . saw . . . got
   (have gotten)
I 4. Mike has applied . . . (a few months ago)
   (applied)
C 5. elected . . . (last month)
I 6. experienced . . . (lately)
   (have experienced)
C 7. (By the end of the meeting) . . . had reached

I 8. has . . . graduated . . . (in June)
(finally graduated)
I 9. am living . . . (since) I was
(have been living)
C 10. was . . . called . . . tried . . . (a few minutes ago) . . .
got

APPENDIX EXERCISE C13 Page 107

I 1. will be trim
(will be trimmed)
C 2. is made
I 3. robbed
(was robbed)
I 4. were describing
(were described)
C 5. has been changed . . . have been filled
I 6. have given
(have been given)
C 7. was cooked . . . was brought
I 8. was accepted
(was accepted by)
I 9. will . . . be allowed . . . have . . . been pay
(have . . . been paid)
C 10. is being held . . . will be posted

APPENDIX EXERCISE C14 Page 108

I 1. won
(was won)
C 2. started
I 3. placed
(were placed)
I 4. selected
(were selected)
C 5. opened
I 6. expected
(was expected)
C 7. amused
I 8. announced
(were announced)
I 9. knocked . . . fell off
(was knocked)
C 10. lasted

APPENDIX REVIEW EXERCISE (C7–C14) Page 109

I 1. *(may have)*
C 2.
I 3. *(were washed and chopped up)*
I 4. *(have drunk)*
I 5. *(has not taken)*
I 6. *(expected)*
I 7. *(was founded)*
C 8.
C 9.
I 10. *(had paid)*
I 11. *(am trying)*
I 12. *(had managed)*
C 13.
C 14.
I 15. *(was interviewed)*

APPENDIX EXERCISE C15 Page 110

I 1. (Each) exhibits
(exhibit)
C 2. (Both) children . . . (various) assignments
C 3. (single) scoop . . . (two) scoops

I 4. (several) pills (every) days
(day)
C 5. (an) . . . time . . . (many) students
I 6. (Various) plans . . . (a) . . . centers
(center)
I 7. (Every) times . . . (several) acquaintances
(time)
I 8. (single) serving . . . (one) people
(person)
C 9. (One) incident . . . (many) misunderstandings
I 10. (several) candidates . . . (each) ones
(one)

APPENDIX EXERCISE C16 Page 111

C 1. (Many) applicants
I 2. (amount) . . . people
(number)
C 3. (Few) suggestions . . . (little) help
I 4. (more) opportunities . . . (less) restrictions
(fewer)
I 5. (much) . . . assurances
(many)
C 6. (number) . . . facts
I 7. (less) concern . . . (much) . . . bills
(many)
C 8. (fewer) men . . . women
I 9. (many) . . . problems . . . (little)
(few)
C 10. (amount) . . . paper

APPENDIX EXERCISE C17 Page 112

I 1. (Him) . . . (me)
(He and I)
C 2. (We) . . . (them) . . . (they) . . . (us)
I 3. (you) . . . (I), (I) . . . (they)
(you . . . me)
C 4. (He) . . . (she) . . . (us) . . . (we)
I 5. (You) . . . (I) . . . (he) . . . (her)
(him . . . her)
I 6. (It) . . . (we)
(for us students)
C 7. (She) . . . (I) . . . (it) to (her) . . . (I) . . . (she)
I 8. (They) . . . (you) . . . (I) . . . (I) . . . (we)
(you and me)
C 9. (It) . . . (us) . . . (it) . . . (him) . . . (her)
I 10. (They) . . . (you) . . . (I)
(you and me)

APPENDIX EXERCISE C18 Page 114

I 1. (our) . . . (ours)
(our teammates)
C 2. (your) . . . (mine)
C 3. (his) . . . (hers)
I 4. (her) . . . (my)
(mine)
C 5. (Your) . . . (my)
I 6. (theirs)
(their offices)
I 7. (my) . . . (your)
(yours)
C 8. (his) . . . (hers)
I 9. (ours) . . . (theirs)
(our keys)
C 10. (your) . . . (hers) . . . (her) . . . (yours)

APPENDIX EXERCISE C19 Page 115

I 1. <u>Papers</u> . . . (it)
(them)
C 2. <u>party</u> . . . (my) <u>neighbors</u> . . . (they) . . . (it)
I 3. <u>Everyone</u> . . . (you)
(he or she wants)
I 4. <u>concert</u> . . . (we) . . . (our) . . . (them)
(it)
C 5. <u>sunshine</u> . . . (I) . . . (it) . . .(my)
I 6. <u>man</u> . . . <u>problem</u> . . . (he) . . . (it) . . . (herself)
(himself)
I 7. (My) <u>friend</u> . . . <u>book</u> . . . (she) . . . (I) . . . (her)
(it)
C 8. (Your) <u>brothers</u> . . . <u>money</u> . . . (they) . . . (you) . . .
(it) . . . (yourself)
I 9. <u>person</u> . . . (their)
(her or his)
I 10. (Your) <u>classmates</u> . . . (yourselves)
(themselves)

APPENDIX REVIEW EXERCISE (C15–C19) Page 115

I 1. (many times)
C 2.
C 3.
I 4. (He and she)
C 5.
C 6.
I 7. (them)
I 8. (to you and me)
I 9. (few of them)
C 10.
I 11. (various needs)
C 12.
I 13. (theirs)
I 14. (fewer calories)
C 15.

APPENDIX EXERCISE C20 Page 116

I 1. *extreme* describes *humid*
humid describes *condition*
(*extremely*)
C 2. *hungry* describes *baby*
quite describes *plaintively*
plaintively describes *wailed*
I 3. *real* describes *exciting*
exciting describes *movie*
unexpected describes *ending*
(*really*)
C 4. *striking* describes *workers*
slowly and *deliberately* describe *marched*
locked describes *gates*
front describes *gates*
I 5. *complex* describes *issue*
thoroughly describes *studied*
difficultly describes *decision*
(*difficult*)
C 6. *parking* describes *lot*
recently describes *had . . . been resurfaced*
thick and *black* describe *asphalt*
I 7. *extremely* describes *cautious*
cautious describes *proceeded*
totally describes *acceptable*
acceptable describes *outcome*
(*cautiously*)

I 8. *rather* describes *suddenly*
suddenly describes *decided*
considerable describes *alter*
(*considerably*)
C 9. *large* and *white* describe *building*
circular describes *driveway*
main describes *office*
I 10. *brilliantly* describes *idea*
supposed describes *shortcut*
(*brilliant*)

APPENDIX EXERCISE C21 Page 119

I 1. *immediately* decribes *return*
(*return the necklace immediately*)
C 2. *serious* describes *man*
always describes *works*
diligently describes *works*
C 3. *worried* describes *mother*
gently describes *scolded*
little describes *girl*
I 4. *often* describes *uses*
(*often uses*)
I 5. *attentive* describes *lifeguard*
quickly describes *jumped*
(*attentive lifeguard*)
C 6. *clearly* describes *explain*
I 7. *carefully* describes *studied*
monthly describes *report*
(*carefully studied*)
C 8. *skillfully* describes *questioned*
hostile describes *witness*
I 9. *always* describes *cannot remember*
(*cannot always remember*)
I 10. *suddenly* describes *dropped*
local describes *people*
chilly describes *weather*
(*local people*)

APPENDIX EXERCISE C22 Page 121

C 1. (fast-moving) line
fast-moving describes *line*
I 2. (satisfying) customers
satisfying describes *customers*
(*satisfied*)
I 3. people . . . (shocked) . . . (disturbed) news
shocked describes *people*
disturbed describes *news*
(*disturbing*)
C 4. (delighted) girl . . . (unexpected) gift
delighted describes *girl*
unexpected describes *gift*
I 5. (depressed) situation
depressed describes *situation*
(*depressing*)
I 6. (snow-capped) mountains . . . (charmed) village
snow-capped describes *mountains*
charmed describes *village*
(*charming*)
C 7. (annoying) guest . . . (frustrated) host
annoying described *guest*
frustrated describes *host*
I 8. (correcting) papers . . . (waiting) students
correcting describes *papers*
waiting describes *students*
(*corrected*)

C   9. (unidentified) attacker . . . (strolling) couple
   unidentified describes *attacker*
   strolling describes *couple*
I 10. (requesting) room . . . (unobstructing) view
   requesting describes *room*
   unobstructing describes *view*
   (requested . . . unobstructed)

APPENDIX EXERCISE C23   Page 123

I   1. <u>Man</u> . . . <u>hat</u> . . . <u>door</u>
   (A man . . . a . . . hat . . . the door)
C   2. (a) . . . <u>task</u>
I   3. <u>job</u>
   (a part-time job)
C   4.
I   5. <u>feeling</u> . . . <u>event</u>
   (a funny feeling . . . a surprising event)
C   6. (a) <u>van</u> . . . (a) <u>family</u>
I   7. (the) . . . <u>course</u> . . . <u>textbook</u> . . . <u>presentation</u>
   (a textbook . . . a presentation)
I   8. (The) <u>family</u> . . . <u>snake</u> . . . <u>dog</u>
   (a snake . . . a . . . dog)
C   9. (a) . . . <u>opinion</u> . . . (a) <u>situation</u>
C 10.

APPENDIX EXERCISE C24   Page 124

C   1. (an) <u>opportunity</u> . . . (a) <u>one-time</u>
I   2. (a) <u>mistake</u> . . . (a) <u>honest</u>
   (an honest)
C   3. (a) <u>hotel</u> . . . (a) <u>jacuzzi</u> . . . (a) <u>sauna</u> . . . (a) <u>heated</u>
I   4. (a) <u>honor</u> . . . (a) <u>guest</u> . . . (a) <u>important</u>
   (an honor . . . an important)
C   5. (a) <u>once-in-a-lifetime</u> . . . (a) <u>faraway</u>
I   6. (a) <u>usual occurrence</u> . . . (a) <u>unusual</u>
   (an unusual)
C   7. (a) <u>colorful</u> . . . (a) <u>hand-painted</u> . . . (a) <u>helium</u>
I   8. (an) <u>euphoric</u> . . . (an) <u>huge</u>
   (a euphoric . . . a huge)
I   9. (A) <u>person</u> . . . (a) <u>X</u> . . . (a) <u>signature</u> . . .
   (a) <u>document</u>
   (an X)
C 10. (a) <u>traditional</u> . . . (a) <u>unicorn</u> . . . (a) <u>helpless</u>

APPENDIX EXERCISE C25   Page 125

I   1. (a) . . . <u>uniforms</u>
   (a . . . uniform)
C   2. (a) <u>notebook</u> . . . (a) <u>textbook</u>
I   3. (a) . . . <u>house</u> . . . (a) . . . <u>pool</u> . . . (a) . . .
   <u>balconies</u> . . . (a) . . . <u>views</u>
   (a . . . balcony . . . a . . . view . . . balcony or balconies
   . . . views . . . balconies)
I   4. (an) . . . <u>theories</u>
   (an . . . theory)
C   5. (a) <u>computer</u>, (a) <u>phone</u>, (a) <u>table</u>
I   6. (a) . . . <u>stories</u>
   (a . . . story)
I   7. (a) . . . <u>dress</u>, (a) . . . <u>shoes</u>, (a) . . . <u>purse</u> . . . (a) . . .
   <u>earrings</u>
   (shoes . . . earrings)
C   8. (a) . . . <u>reason</u>
I   9. (a) . . . <u>biscuits</u>
   (biscuits)
C 10. (a) <u>secretary</u>

APPENDIX EXERCISE C26   Page 126

I   1. (a) . . . <u>ride</u> . . . (an) . . . <u>continent</u>
   (the African continent)
C   2. (a) <u>movie</u> . . . (a) . . . <u>ending</u>
I   3. (a) . . . <u>cloud</u> . . . (a) <u>sky</u>
   (the sky)
I   4. (The) <u>spacecraft</u> . . . (a) <u>planet</u>
   (the planet)
I   5. (The) <u>teacher</u> . . . (a) <u>middle</u> . . . (the) <u>classroom</u> . . .
   (the) <u>students</u>
   (the middle)
C   6. (an) <u>idea</u> . . . (a) <u>topic</u> . . . (an) . . . <u>paper</u>
I   7. (a) . . . <u>hotel</u> . . . (a) . . . <u>time</u>
   (the . . . hotel . . . the . . . time)
I   8. (A) <u>hat</u> . . . (a) . . . <u>hat</u>
   (The hat)
I   9. (a) <u>prize</u> . . . (a) . . . essay (the) . . . <u>contest</u>
   (the . . . essay)
I 10. (the) . . . <u>man</u> . . . (a) nose . . . (a) . . . nose
   (the nose)

APPENDIX REVIEW EXERCISE (C20–C26)   Page 127

I   1. *(an unbelievably)*
C   2.
I   3. *(often misplaces)*
I   4. *(The engine . . . a funny noise or funny noises)*
C   5.
C   6.
I   7. *(substantial benefits)*
C   8.
I   9. *(a nearby university)*
C 10.
I 11. *(a delight)*
I 12. *(unmade beds . . . unwashed dishes)*
C 13.
I 14. *(swiftly collected)*
I 15. *(the . . . principal . . . a speech)*

AUDIO CD TRACKING LIST

Track	Page	Activity
CD 1		
1		CD 1 Program Information
2		CD 1 title
3	1	Writing Diagnostic Pre-Test Directions
4	2	Question 1 Reading Directions
5	2	Question 1 Listening Passage
6	2	Question 1
7	3	Question 2
8	12	Writing Exercise 2, Question 1
9	13	Writing Exercise 2, Question 2
10	13	Writing Exercise 2, Question 3
11	29	Writing Review Exercise (Skills 1–8) Reading Directions
12	29	Writing Review Exercise (Skills 1–8) Listening Passage
13	29	Writing Review Exercise (Skills 1–8) Question
14	51	Writing Post-Test Directions
15	52	Question 1 Reading Directions
16	52	Question 1 Listening Passage
17	52	Question 1
18	53	Question 2
19	54	Writing Mini-Test 1 Directions
20	55	Reading Directions
21	55	Listening Passage
22	55	Question
23	56	Writing Mini-Test 2 Directions
24	57	Question
25	58	Writing Mini-Test 3 Directions
26	59	Reading Directions
27	59	Listening Passage
28	59	Question
29	60	Writing Mini-Test 4 Directions
30	61	Question

Track	Page	Activity
CD 2		
1		CD 2 Program Introduction
2	62	Writing Mini-Test 5 Directions
3	63	Reading Directions
4	63	Listening Passage
5	63	Question
6	64	Writing Mini-Test 6 Directions
7	65	Question
8	66	Writing Mini-Test 7 Directions
9	67	Reading Directions
10	67	Listening Passage
11	67	Question
12	68	Writing Mini-Test 8 Directions
13	69	Question
14	70	Writing Complete Test 1 Directions
15	71	Question 1: Reading Directions
16	71	Question 1: Listening Passage
17	71	Question 1
18	72	Question 2
19	73	Writing Complete Test 2 Directions
20	74	Question 1: Reading Directions
21	74	Question 1: Listening Passage
22	74	Question 1
23	75	Question 2

Single User License Agreement: